T0319032

Cambridge Elements

Elements in Historical Theory and Practice
edited by
Daniel Woolf
Queen's University, Ontario

ARCHAEOLOGY AS HISTORY

Telling Stories from a Fragmented Past

Catherine J. Frieman
Australian National University

CAMBRIDGE
UNIVERSITY PRESS

CAMBRIDGE
UNIVERSITY PRESS

Shaftesbury Road, Cambridge CB2 8EA, United Kingdom

One Liberty Plaza, 20th Floor, New York, NY 10006, USA

477 Williamstown Road, Port Melbourne, VIC 3207, Australia

314–321, 3rd Floor, Plot 3, Splendor Forum, Jasola District Centre,
New Delhi – 110025, India

103 Penang Road, #05–06/07, Visioncrest Commercial, Singapore 238467

Cambridge University Press is part of Cambridge University Press & Assessment,
a department of the University of Cambridge.

We share the University's mission to contribute to society through the pursuit of
education, learning and research at the highest international levels of excellence.

www.cambridge.org
Information on this title: www.cambridge.org/9781009055567

DOI: 10.1017/9781009052412

First published 2023

A catalogue record for this publication is available from the British Library.

ISBN 978-1-009-05556-7 Paperback
ISSN 2634-8616 (online)
ISSN 2634-8608 (print)

Archaeology as History

Telling Stories from a Fragmented Past

Elements in Historical Theory and Practice

DOI: 10.1017/9781009052412
First published online: July 2023

Catherine J. Frieman
Australian National University

Author for correspondence: Catherine J. Frieman,
catherine.frieman@anu.edu.au

Abstract: This Element focusses on how archaeologists construct narratives of past people and environments from the complex and fragmented archaeological record. In keeping with its position in a series of historiography, it considers how we make meaning from things and places, with an emphasis on changing practices over time and the questions archaeologists have and can ask of the archaeological record. It aims to provide readers with a reflexive and comprehensive overview of what it is that archaeologists do with the archaeological record, how that translates into specific stories or narratives about the past, and the limitations or advantages of these when trying to understand past worlds. The goal is to shift the reader's perspective of archaeology away from seeing it as a primarily data-gathering field to a clearer understanding of how archaeologists make and use the data they uncover.

This Element also has a video abstract: Cambridge.org/Frieman_abstract

Keywords: archaeological method, archaeological theory, history of archaeology, activist archaeology, introduction to archaeology

ISBNs: 9781009055567 (PB), 9781009052412 (OC)
ISSNs: 2634-8616 (online), 2634-8608 (print)

Contents

Introduction

In its broadest sense, archaeology is the study of human society through the lens of our material and natural environments, that is, the things people made and used, the world they inhabited, and the traces their practices left on that world. For much of the human past, archaeological material offers us our only insight into who people were and how they lived. Writing is a very recent invention on the scale of human evolution, was never universally used, and only in recent centuries has been directed to documenting (some of) the mundanities of (some people's) daily life (in some parts of the world for some periods of time). Nevertheless, and despite the impression certain TV programmes might give, archaeologists do not just concern themselves with this deep past of a world without writing. Archaeological research coexists with historical studies because it looks at fundamentally different data with different methods and different motivations.

Nearly all the questions we want to answer about the past and the people who lived then – the journalist's standard set of who, what, where, when, how, and why – can be (and have been) at least partially answered by close analysis of the things people made and used, the places they occupied, the structures they built, and the way their bodies reflected social practices and habitual activities. Some of these questions are more accessible than others. Nearly seventy years ago, the Oxford professor Christopher Hawkes proposed a sequence of interpretation that has subsequently come to be known as 'Hawkes' Ladder of Inference'.[1] Following Hawkes, archaeologists should find it relatively straightforward to infer how artefacts were made and of what materials; it is a bit more difficult to infer the economic systems through which these objects were traded and valued; it becomes quite hard to infer aspects of the social and political organisation of past societies; and it should be nearly impossible to infer past cosmologies and religious practices. In fact, in the intervening decades we have developed methods, both scientific and interpretative, to access all of these domains; but with each new method or approach new questions assert themselves.

The increasing complexity of our methods is unsurprising because the *archaeological record* (the assemblage of things, natural and anthropogenic, studied by archaeologists) itself is irreparably fragmented. The material residue of the past is not only incomplete; it is unknowably incomplete: we do not (and cannot) know what is missing, from where, and in what quantities (although sometimes we can develop some good hypotheses about why). Philosophers of the historical sciences (and some archaeologists) have agonised about the *underdetermination* of the discipline, that is, that our data's

---

[1] Hawkes (1954).

innate fragmentation means that we cannot make incontrovertible inferences about the people and worlds of the past.[2] If we assume there was a singular truth of the past that we are attempting to view around the gaps in the archaeological record, then we are indeed in trouble; but this is not the only perspective.[3] Indeed, one can argue that there are many pasts because different cultures and individuals have different personal, communal, dominant, and subordinate histories which they tell and remember in a variety of ways.[4]

Most archaeologists tend to take a more pragmatic approach. Since our data are complicated and fragmented, our methods must also be complicated and our interpretations able to cope with uncertainty.[5] Archaeology is a sort of magpie science because of the way we lift, adapt, and reinvent methods, bodies of theory, and scientific models from a range of other disciplines from history to sociology to anthropology to biology to chemistry to physics and beyond.[6] Moreover, if we let go of the idea that there is a singular truth to the past, we are free to embrace instead the more challenging idea that our models of the past are composed in the present through complex relationships between individual training, the communities of practitioners with whom we collaborate, long-standing (often regional) disciplinary traditions, and the material residue of past people's lives and practice.[7] This approach allows us to reflect on the process we engage in as archaeologists to consider how the questions we pose of the past affect the methods we choose to apply, the results we achieve, and the stories we are able to tell.

Here, I use the framework of 'telling stories' to emphasise that archaeological narratives are constructed as plausible throughlines to connect the variety of archaeological data and many complementary sources of information.[8] As new data are uncovered or emerge from new analytical techniques or interpretative approaches, the story will shift. Moreover, archaeological stories about the past coexist (and sometimes entwine) with historical narratives, oral history, and other traditions of interpretation. These are also domains with which archaeologists engage and which are becoming increasingly prominent in the field – especially in the case of co-creative work with descendant communities. The point here is that the fragmentation of the archaeological record, the enormous variety of methodological and theoretical tools we have developed (or borrowed) to interpret it, and the very different traditions in which global archaeologists are trained all contribute to a diversity of pasts, a diversity of truths, and a diversity of stories that connect the dots of broken pottery, crumbling buildings, and burnt seeds.

---

[2] Chapman and Wylie (2016: 15–31); Turner (2005, 2007).   [3] Currie (2018, 2021).
[4] Nabokov (2002); Olivier (2011).   [5] Gero (2007).   [6] Frieman (2021: 3).
[7] Gero (1985); Hodder (1999) cf. Latour and Woolgar (1979).   [8] Pluciennik (1999).

This Element seeks to explore these diverse approaches to the study of the past, emphasising that the data archaeologists present to the world are not innately meaningful but constructed through careful analysis and traditions of interpretation. It is broken into five sections, each roughly addressing the questions where, what, when, who, and why (the 'how' is implicit throughout). First, I discuss the ways archaeologists study places and landscapes, building information from layers of earth and patterns of land division. Next, I explore the long history of artefact studies and the role of material analysis in the construction of archaeological narratives. Following that, I look at how archaeologists construct chronologies through both close analysis of materials and increasingly sophisticated scientific methods. Then, I ask how we study people – both their bodies and their societies – and tell stories at the level of the individual. Finally, I focus on the impact of archaeological work in the present and how the methods of archaeology can make space for marginalised people to speak loudly and tell their own histories. A brief conclusion draws these various threads together.

In weaving this particular narrative, I bring together case studies from around the world and from myriad periods in human history – from the evolution of hominins to the twenty-first century. I draw on insights from Black, Indigenous, and other marginalised or minoritised archaeologists to emphasise the diversity of approaches to the past and how high the stakes are for getting it right. Archaeology and archaeologists may often study a world long disappeared, but we exist and work in a present where issues of history, truth, and sovereignty remain contested.[9] In this context, I feel it is more important now than ever to consider the tools we use to find and reconstruct the past and to reflect on which stories we choose to tell.

1 Telling Stories about Places

If I asked you to picture an archaeologist, chances are you would immediately think of a person in a trench with a brush or trowel excavating the earth. Depending on what TV programmes you had watched, you might think of a person carrying mysterious pinging machines as they stride evenly across a field or down a hill slope (Figure 1). This impression is not entirely incorrect, as archaeologists have a long-standing interest in the places past people built and occupied. We seek to study these at a range of scales – from the microscopic traces of past practice to a wider landscape; and we have developed a variety of methodological tools to create information about the past from layers of dirt,

---

[9] Stahl (2022).

Figure 1 Archaeologists surveying a prehistoric monument.
© South East Kernow Archaeological Survey (SEKAS).

ruined monuments, standing buildings, and the patterns of construction and activity visible in a wider region.

Excavation is our best-known method. During an archaeological excavation, archaeologists will open a trench and dig downwards with care and precision. The reason we go to all this effort is because excavation offers us a uniquely fine-grained insight into how people occupied any given place over a sequence of decades, centuries, or millennia. While nineteenth- and early twentieth-century excavations were aimed at finding (and often then stealing) valuable treasure from tombs or ancient cities, most archaeologists today find more value in broken bits of pottery, ratty stone tools, and old floor surfaces or foundations because these offer insights into habitual practices and daily life (see Section 2). Even in periods with copious written texts, many people and their lives are invisible – usually poor people, women, children, and enslaved people; but archaeological research allows us to look directly at the tools they made and used, the food they ate, and the homes they built and lived in, as well as the ways they resisted domination.[10]

For example, in Africa, archaeological excavation on sites dating to the colonial era allows us to glimpse the complex relationships and developments of African society beyond the narrow, often racist, lens of colonial European

---

[10] Orser and Funari (2001).

writing. The archaeologist Shadreck Chirikure, for example, uses archaeological data to demonstrate how southern African people engaged in complex and culturally contingent ways with the colonial powers who controlled the Indian Ocean trade network in the sixteenth and seventeenth centuries. He notes that imported European and Chinese ceramics are found in large numbers in excavations of Portuguese trade markets (*feira*) but not at high-status local settlements, such as Great Zimbabwe, because this exogenous pottery lay outside the local cultural logic, not being useful in significant cultural practices, such as beer-making for ancestors, food service, or rain-making ceremonies.[11]

Our excavation methods have developed slowly and regionally over the history of archaeology, with resultant variation in practice; and there is no one correct way to excavate (despite what many individual archaeologists think). Trenches, for example, are sized to fit the research questions of a project as well as legal and ethical requirements alongside constraints, such as the nature and extent of a given site, its depth, and the safety of the excavation team. So, some may be *open area excavations* with tens or hundreds of metres square of topsoil removed, while others may be small squares 50 cm or 1 m on a side, sometimes referred to as *shovel test pits*, *test pits*, or *sondages*. Excavation is painstaking and systematic, though not always slow: professional archaeologists in particular must operate precisely but at speed to meet contracted development targets, and university-affiliated archaeologists also often have only a limited time frame to answer their research questions before they must close up their trenches and return to their campuses.

No matter the available time, good archaeologists remove layers of sediment with care, almost always attempting to follow *stratigraphic layers*. Drawing on insights from geology, nineteenth-century archaeologists observed that deposits tend to form in layers, with the oldest layers lowest down; this is called the *law of superposition*.[12] So, when a site is excavated, the material lowest in the sequence should be older than the material closer to the surface (Figure 2). As archaeological excavation removes *in situ* data from their *context* and *associations* (i.e., the stratigraphic layer from which data were recovered and the artefacts and materials that were deposited or formed alongside them), archaeologists are careful to excavate only enough material to answer their research questions or to give full indication of the level of significance of a given site or area.

Not all material is preserved to the same extent, and sites may be affected by a variety of natural and cultural *site formation processes*, from erosion or animal burrowing to reoccupation or looting.[13] These processes can disrupt site

---

[11] Chirikure (2014).   [12] Rowley-Conwy (2007: 57–60).   [13] Schiffer (1987).

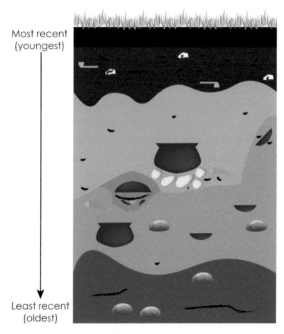

Most recent
(youngest)

Least recent
(oldest)

Figure 2 A schematic vertical profile of an excavation showing the stratigraphy.

stratigraphy, remove or destroy materials, and damage archaeological features in other ways. Geological processes like hill-slope erosion, earthquakes, rock falls in caves, or landslides can also result in *inverted stratigraphy*, with older material resting on top of more recent layers. The variable decay processes affecting archaeological materials (a series of complex processes classed together as *taphonomy*) also shape what materials are preserved and in what manner.[14] Reconstructing all these processes is necessary in order to understand the development of a given archaeological site, the materials we would expect to see preserved, and how best to interpret what we do find. This typically entails considerable interdisciplinary collaboration, including geological and geomorphological analysis (see the box 'Environmental Archaeologies and Geoarchaeology').

ENVIRONMENTAL ARCHAEOLOGIES AND GEOARCHAEOLOGY

Understanding the way people occupied and used a given landscape or site requires us to understand its natural and geological context. Since the middle of the twentieth century, archaeology has seen an explosion in environmental subfields, including *archaeobotany* (the study of macrobotanical remains, i.e.,

---

[14] Lyman (2010).

seeds or plant parts, sometimes including *anthracology*, the study of charcoal), *zooarchaeology* (the study of faunal remains), *archaeomalacology* (the study of invertebrates, especially molluscs), *palynology* (the study of pollen), and *geomorphology* (the study of landforms and landform evolution). Many geoarchaeologists are also closely involved in remote sensing surveys, including *geochemical* and *geophysical* survey methods. Collectively, these approaches allow us to reconstruct the formation processes that shaped the archaeological record, to delineate the *palaeoenvironments* of regions or specific archaeological sites, and to clarify how people were engaging with plants, animals, and their local geological environment.

For example, in a series of recent papers, the geoarchaeologist Elle Grono and colleagues (many with environmental archaeology specialisms) reconstructed the occupation and formation of three Holocene sites in Vietnam.[15] At Thach Lac, a 2 m high shell mound dated to 5000–4100 BP, they undertook a micromorphological analysis (i.e., creating thin sections of the stratigraphic profile to study microscopically) to develop a fine-grained sequence of occupation and abandonment, as well as natural soil formation over the site's thousand years of use. At Lo Gach, by contrast, Grono and colleagues used a similar micromorphological analysis combined with archaeobotanical data to identify outside working areas within a Neolithic (c.3300–2400 BP) settlement, a significant arena of domestic activity in the tropics that is otherwise archaeologically invisible. At the slightly earlier settlement of Loc Giang (4070–3150 BP), their analysis in combination with other environmental data allowed them to identify the remains of a sequence of dwellings, both ground-level and raised on piles, as well as layers of organic refuse that could be linked to animal management.

While we rarely actually use brushes and tiny picks to excavate (we save these for particularly special contexts, such as intact artefacts or burials), archaeologists take immense care and precision in excavation, choosing among a variety of tools (trowels, mattocks, shovels, etc.) and approaches in response to the soil conditions, delicacy of the archaeological record, local best practice, and levels of knowledge about the site under excavation. Where there is little information about the possible stratigraphy or if it is not clear if the stratigraphy relates to cultural events, an archaeologist will often remove thin *spits* or *arbitrary layers* (level layers of an even thickness – often 5 cm or 10 cm – of sediment) within a stratigraphic layer

---

[15] Grono, Friesem, Lam et al. (2022); Grono, Friesem, Wood et al. (2022); Grono, Piper et al. (2022).

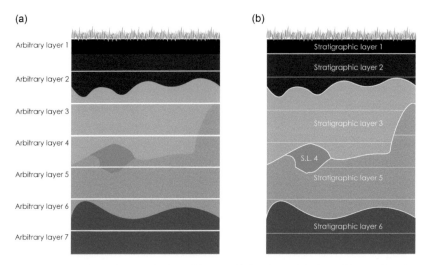

Figure 3 A schematic vertical profile: (a) divided up only by arbitrary levels;
(b) divided by arbitrary levels within the stratigraphic levels.

that may be flat (Figure 3(a)) or follow the undulations of the stratigraphy in order to avoid mixing or digging through multiple layers at once, (Figure 3(b)). At sites where stratigraphic layers represent long periods of accumulation, data from spits excavated within them can offer more chronological control. In some parts of the world or on sites and/or under weather conditions where the stratigraphy is hard to discern, all excavation proceeds in spits, with the stratigraphy determined after-wards based on the trench's *vertical profile* (sometimes termed its *section*). This is less than ideal since, if stratigraphic layers are not horizontal but form at an angle, it can risk an archaeologist cutting through and mixing material from multiple separate stratigraphic layers in a single arbitrary layer, as in Figure 3(a).

One important tool to interpret stratigraphic sequences is the *Harris matrix* (sometimes known as the *Harris–Winchester matrix*). It was developed in the 1970s by Edward Harris during the excavations at the medieval town of Winchester, UK as a tool to help make sense of the deep and complex stratigraphy he and his colleagues encountered.[16] Essentially, a Harris matrix offers us a tool to navigate and diagram complex layers of archaeological deposits in order to understand the sequence in which those layers were deposited (Figure 4). Making a Harris matrix is not always easy. Sometimes the layers stack neatly one on top of the next (Figure 4(a)), but more often the interfaces between them are obscured by holes for posts, wall foundations, or pits (Figure 4(a) and 4(c)). To make the matrix, we follow the *law of stratigraphic succession*, that is, we only

---

[16] Harris (1979).

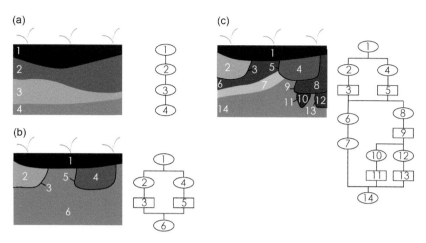

Figure 4 Composing a Harris matrix from archaeological stratigraphy:
(a) simple matrix showing four layers deposited in succession;
(b) a matrix in which two pits are cut into deposit 6; (c) a more complex matrix
that shows multiple intercutting pits and successive layers of deposits
(redrawn with changes after Bibby 1993: fig. 7).

record the stratification between a given *context* or *stratigraphic unit* (an unbound *deposit* or the *fill* or *cut* of a pit) based on the unit directly before and after it in the sequence and with which it has physical contact, without regard to the rest. This means we are not always able to determine the order of features like the two pits in Figure 4(b), but we can determine each pit was cut into deposit 6 and is cut or covered by deposit 1. As in Figure 4, many archaeologists use symbols like rectangles or circles to distinguish between fills and deposits on the one hand and cuts on the other. This is because fills and deposits, being layers of sediment, can have other samples associated, like artefacts, environmental samples, or dates, while cuts, being the residue of action (i.e., the act of digging out a hollow for a pit, posthole, etc.), do not. The system of symbols helps keep records in order as a complex excavation progresses.

A major part of any excavation is record-keeping. Until the later twentieth century, most excavation records took the form of field notes in the project director's notebook (Figure 5). Field notes in archaeology are usually reasonably impersonal descriptions of the excavation process, observations of the soil, stratigraphy, and artefacts revealed, as well as sketches of the in-progress excavation, interesting finds, or puzzling features (see the box 'Archaeological Illustration'). Some include observations on the excavation team and their dynamics, the weather from day to day, relevant stories or information shared by local visitors to the site, as well as other more discursive information. Alongside these more personal

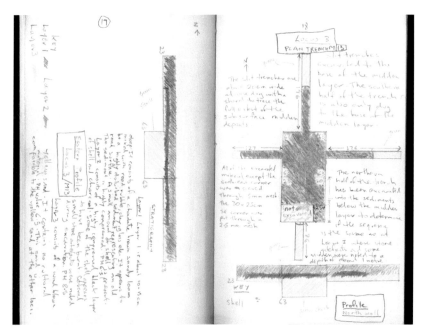

Figure 5 A site director's notebook. By permission of Australian National University (ANU) Collections and the School of Archaeology and Anthropology.

narratives of excavation, as types of analysis have multiplied and relational databases have become standard, more systematic and interlinked records are frequently produced. Uniquely numbered forms are filled out for each spit and stratigraphic unit, as well as any samples taken (e.g., for environmental analysis, radiocarbon dating, etc.) and any *small finds*, datable or rare implements that deserve special analytical attention. Separate records are also kept that list all the excavated contexts, the various measurements recorded, and the illustrations made during the excavation. These provide important tools to cross-reference data between forms, notebooks, finds bags, drawings, and samples so that all associated data remain associated even as some material is sent off to specialists for analysis.

ARCHAEOLOGICAL ILLUSTRATION

Archaeology is a very visual field and has been since its emergence as a discipline.[17] Archaeologists spend a lot of time taking photographs, making maps, and creating illustrations, including drawings of excavations, features, objects, and archaeological sites. Most contemporary archaeological

---

[17] Moser (2012).

drawing is technical rather than artistic, with established conventions for rendering three-dimensional objects into two dimensions in such a way that important features are clearly communicated to knowledgeable viewers.[18] Learning scale drawing to document the *plan* (top-down extent or map) of an excavated feature or trench and its *section* (a square-on vertical profile of an excavated feature, deposit, or trench) is a key skill taught in most archaeology programmes. Buildings archaeologists similarly draw to-scale sections to document structural stratigraphy (as in Figure 6), as well as to-scale top-down plans and three-dimensional *planometric drawings* of the structures they study to record the presence and articulation of various architectural features.

Drawings are among the most valuable records in excavation archives because they allow later scholars to reconstruct the excavation process and the interpretations archaeologists were making at the moment when a site, layer, feature, or significant object was encountered. For example, Gillespie demonstrated that maps and plans of Complex A at the Olmec site of La Venta (Mexico) drawn during its initial excavation in the 1950s contained significant information about the site's occupation and the relationship between social practices and its architectural monuments that subsequent research had overlooked.[19] Although cartographic drawings have largely been replaced by digital maps – many produced with *geographical information system* (*GIS*) software packages (e.g., QGIS) rather than more artistic tools – archaeologists are well aware that spatial analysis and mapping are analytical rather than objective processes.[20]

Photography complements hand-drawn illustrations, adding texture and colour, as well as occasionally catching features not noted or recognised as significant by the excavation team.[21] These photographs are composed with site archives in mind and typically include scale bars and north arrows to situate them in space. In recent years, drones have been used to capture plan photographs of large trenches and excavation features; and 3D models composed with specialist software from hundreds or thousands of individual digital photographs are also becoming more common. Other digital methods for imaging archaeological materials, sites, and features include laser scanning, *photogrammetry* (the construction of 3D models from photographs), or *reflectance transformation imaging* (*RTI*) to record surface features and

---

[18] For example, Adkins and Adkins (1989); Small (2013); Steiner and Allason-Jones (2005).
[19] Gillespie (2011).   [20] Gillings et al. (2018, 2020).
[21] Dorrell (1994); Fisher (2009a, 2009b).

textures in high definition, as well as image enhancement with software tools like Xshade and DStretch.[22]

Although photographs are quicker to produce than drawings, analysis by Morgan and Wright suggests that the cognitive work we engage in while drawing is not well replicated by digital recording methods; so, the persistence of these less efficient methods can be explained by their evident value as interpretative tools that help to disentangle a messy archaeological record.[23]

The archaeological record exists above as well as below the ground. Standing monuments are some of the most visible, and thus most investigated, sites. These include old buildings, bridges and other infrastructure, stone circles or tombs, and even large earthen monuments like bank and ditch arrangements or agricultural terraces. Many of the earliest antiquaries, the intellectual ancestors of archaeologists, were fascinated by these sorts of visible traces of the past; and early antiquarian writing described European prehistoric monuments like burial mounds and standing stones as well as more recent structures, such as medieval churches.[24] As western European powers colonised Eurasia, Africa, and the wider world, these early archaeologists were part of the colonial movement, mapping sites and cities, interpreting their histories, and looting them to enrich museums in London, Paris, and elsewhere (see the box 'Archaeology and Colonial Expansion').

ARCHAEOLOGY AND COLONIAL EXPANSION

When Indiana Jones shouts 'that belongs in a museum' about a medieval gold cross or Killmonger points to the artefacts in a London museum taken from African people by British soldiers, they are accurately portraying the practice and results of archaeology's long-standing colonial entanglement and persistent cultural violence.[25] Looting as a nationalist project is an established element of European imperial expansion and one in which archaeological excavation has played a central role. Indeed, as archaeology emerged as a distinct discipline within the context of European nationalism and hegemonic colonialism, it was rapidly put to the service of consolidating control and asserting power over colonial places.[26] This process included the excavation of sites in colonised areas

---

[22] For example, Evans and Mourad (2018); Jones et al. (2015).
[23] Morgan and Wright (2018).   [24] Schnapp (1996).
[25] *Black Panther*, directed by Ryan Coogler, Marvel Studios, 2018; *Indiana Jones and the Last Crusade*, directed by Steven Spielberg, Paramount Pictures, 1989.
[26] Díaz-Andreu García (2007).

and the collection (theft) of ancient materials for European collectors and institutions.

Archaeological survey and excavation practices owe much to nineteenth-century European military men. Christopher Evans draws out the connections between specific British military officers and the emergence of a suite of archaeological techniques – landscape survey, cartography, trenching – as well as specific archaeological and collecting campaigns, among them the launch of the Indian Archaeology Survey in the mid-nineteenth century.[27] Even the traditional structure of excavation campaigns (another military term), with their powerful directors and teams of uncredited excavators (often local workers or, more recently, students), reproduces the hierarchical and extractive logics of colonial invasions.[28] Today, we still grapple with this complex and ugly history, and many archaeologists are taking steps to rebuild the discipline on new, diverse, and community-oriented foundations (Section 5).

We have developed many techniques to study standing monuments, some destructive, some non-destructive (it is a rare community that would let you knock down their church or temple to understand how it was built). The questions we ask of these sites differ depending on the period, region, and local methodological landscape but largely boil down to: how was it built, by whom, with what materials, when, and why?[29] Some of these are easier to answer than others. While earlier monument studies might be described as art historical or typological, in recent years more analytical methods have been developed, chief among these the delineation of phases of activity through stratigraphic analysis. *Stratigraphy* in archaeology is most typically used to describe sequential layers of earth uncovered by excavation, but it has been adopted as a metaphor to describe phases of activity that affect the substance or shape of a standing building. Combined with other methods, it can offer us a fine-grained insight into the chronology, process, and rationale behind the changing shape and functions of structures, as well as into how people were occupying or using that structure. In an anglophone context, this approach is sometimes termed *buildings archaeology*.

As an example, Sánchez-Pardo and colleagues used a stratigraphic approach combined with scientific analysis of specific materials to tease out the construction process, remodelling, and dating of a small church in northern Spain called Santa Comba de Bande. Previous research based on medieval documents had suggested it dated to the seventh century and was Visigothic (i.e., it predated the Islamic invasion of Iberia and the foundation of al-Andalus), but archaeological work on the church

[27] Evans (2014). [28] Leighton (2015). [29] Azkarate (2020).

dated it instead to the Mozarabic period in the later ninth century. Sánchez-Pardo and colleagues used the building's stratigraphy (Figure 6) to identify the earliest construction phases, and mortar samples were taken from these to be dated with optically stimulated luminescence (OSL) and radiocarbon dates were made on sediment samples (for information about these dating techniques, see Section 3). They concluded that the initial construction phases at Santa Comba de Bande in fact took place in the later eighth century. This suggests that this church, with its stylistic mixture of Visigothic and later Mozarabic elements, may have been built by southern Iberian Christians fleeing northwards from the newly established al-Andalus. It demonstrates that earlier architectural styles remained in currency well into the Islamic period in Iberia and that, even from just a few decades after the 711 CE Arab conquest, Islamic art and architectural styles were already circulating beyond al-Andalus.[30]

While sites – both above and below ground – are a major focus of attention, the wider landscape in which they sit provides key information about human activities through time and how those sites were used. *Surveying* has become central to archaeological fieldwork over the last few decades, in both research and professional contexts.[31] Methods can be non-invasive (topographic survey,

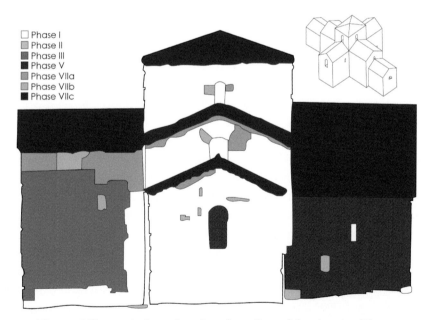

Phase I
Phase II
Phase III
Phase V
Phase VIIa
Phase VIIb
Phase VIIc

Figure 6 The vertical stratigraphy of one face of the church of Santa Comba de Bande, Spain (redrawn with changes after Sánchez-Pardo et al. 2017: fig. 5).

---

[30] Sánchez-Pardo et al. (2017).   [31] Bintliff (2000).

remote sensing, etc.) or destructive (e.g., *test-pitting*, a sampling strategy in which *shovel test pits* or *sondages* are excavated at intervals on a grid or randomly within an area to characterise the archaeological deposits throughout that area).[32] Surveys are cost-effective and efficient ways to learn about the type, age, and significance of any archaeological deposits in an area under investigation and to determine whether large-scale excavation is merited.

Non-invasive survey methods include *surface survey* (sometimes termed *field walking*), that is, traversing a given area in a regular manner (usually by evenly spaced transects) and collecting archaeological material visible on the surface. This material may be retained for analysis or identified and left in the field, depending on the sampling strategy and local laws. Many surveys also collect environmental data, as they indicate the changing vegetation and geomorphology that impact on site formation processes and shape or reflect human activity in a given region. These may be collected by hand (e.g., from shovel test pits) or using tools like *augurs* that allow the collection of a continuous deep profile.

Over the last few decades, *remote sensing* has become a commonly used method of regional survey (Table 1).[33] Depending on the expertise, budget, and experience of the research team (not to mention local geological and topographic conditions), this might include satellite imagery, light-detecting and ranging (LiDAR) systems, ground-penetrating radar (GPR), and/or other geophysical methods. The results depend on the technique used and the ground conditions, but these techniques can yield highly detailed maps of subsurface or near-surface features that archaeologists can begin to interpret and tentatively date or sequence. Geoarchaeologists also apply many of these tools to develop their understanding of the geomorphology and subsurface geology in areas of archaeological interest.[34] However, like all non-invasive methods, remote sensing is only as good as the analyst's experience and expertise. Combining methods provides us with the richest and most accurate data set.

At Talland Barton in Cornwall in the UK, aerial photography suggested the presence of two connected enclosures, tentatively dated to the Iron Age. A geophysical survey using magnetometry located one of the two enclosures (hypothesised to be Romano-British based on its form) but indicated that the other was an artefact of differential plant growth due to erosion on a steep slope rather than an archaeological feature (Figure 7).[35] The magnetometry survey also located a number of different anthropogenic features, including a modern water pipe, a small rectilinear structure of unknown date, and a large ditched field system, tentatively dated to the historic period. Upon excavation, while the enclosure

---

[32] Banning (2002). [33] Parcak (2014); Wiseman and El-Baz (2007). [34] Sarris et al. (2018).
[35] Lewis and Frieman (2017).

Table 1 Major techniques for archaeological remote sensing.

Remote sensing technique type	Name	Basic description of method	Constraints
Aerial imagery methods	Aerial photography (AP)	Vertical and oblique optical images (photographs) of sites and cropmarks taken from kites, drones, and aeroplanes to detect archaeological features and identify their extent and relationships (chronological, functional, etc.).	Highly dependent on local geology and weather conditions, as well as the experience of the analyst in distinguishing archaeological from natural features and correctly identifying them.
	Satellite imaging	Optical and multispectral (MSS, TIMS, etc.) imagery of sites and landscapes taken from space to identify anomalies in the landscape, geology, and vegetation that might indicate archaeological occupation and/or construct digital elevation models of landforms without regard to modern development.	High-resolution imagery can be costly and is only available for some regions, although this is improving with services like Google Earth. Highly dependent on the experience of the analyst in distinguishing archaeological from natural features and correctly identifying them.

| Multispectral scanning (MSS) and thermal infrared multispectral scanning (TIMS) | Electromagnetic and thermal infrared imagery of sites and landscapes taken from space (key collections: Landsat, Spot, Ikonos) to identify archaeological sites and landscapes as well as vegetational and geological formations associated with anthropogenic activity, including past sites or occupations. | High-resolution imagery can be costly and is only available for some regions. Highly dependent on the skill and experience of the analyst and their access to appropriate software packages to resolve the imagery and correctly distinguish archaeological features. |
| Light detecting and ranging (LiDAR) | Topographic modelling of near-surface features by shooting a laser at a surface and measuring the time for it to return to the sensor (mounted on a fixed base station, drone, or aeroplane), allowing high-definition models of subsurface features to be visualised to detect archaeological features and identify their extent and relationships. | Increasingly affordable with drone technology but often limited in extent. High-definition imagery is only available for some regions. Highly dependent on the skill and experience of the analyst and their access to appropriate software packages to resolve and interpret the imagery. |

Table 1 (cont.)

Remote sensing technique type	Name	Basic description of method	Constraints
Ground-based geophysical methods	Ground-penetrating radar (GPR)	An electromagnetic pulse directed into the ground from a mobile sensor reflects off objects and buried features, allowing subsurface features to be detected, located in three dimensions, and identified.	Equipment can be costly and must be carefully maintained. Highly dependent on local geology and hydrology, with non-uniform deposits and very wet or consolidated soils potentially creating too much noise for scans to be read. Highly dependent on the skill and experience of the analyst and their access to appropriate software packages to resolve and interpret scanned data.
	Electrical resistivity	An electric pulse sent between probes in a mobile frame detects the electrical resistivity of the soil in a given location, with patterns of higher and lower resistivity to detect and identify subsurface deposits, including archaeological features (e.g., walls, paths, structures).	Equipment is less expensive than other forms of geophysics but must be carefully maintained. Survey can be extremely time-consuming. Reasonably dependent on local geology, and hydrology, with waterlogged and stony deposits being particularly problematic. Highly dependent on the skill and experience of the analyst and their access to appropriate software packages to resolve and interpret scanned data.

Magnetic prospection (magnetometry)	A sensor (typically a gradiometer, caesium magnetometer, or array of these carried by hand or mounted on one or more carts) measures the local magnetic field to detect and identify magnetic anomalies compared to the total magnetic field strength to identify subsurface deposits, including archaeological features (e.g., ditches, pits, structures, hearths).	Equipment can be costly and must be carefully maintained. Handheld magnetometry survey can be time-consuming and physically strenuous. Somewhat dependent on local geology and hydrology. Highly dependent on the skill and experience of the analyst and their access to appropriate software packages to resolve and interpret scanned data.
Metal detecting	Usually a coil on a long handle that transmits an electromagnetic field into the ground to energise metallic objects which then retransmit their own electromagnetic field, allowing them to be located on an X–Y plane.	The higher the precision, the higher the cost of the equipment. Most equipment does not log points, so data cannot be captured and visualised. Encourages destruction of intact archaeological contexts to remove the isolated metal objects detected.

(a)　　　　　　　　　　　　　　　　　　(b)

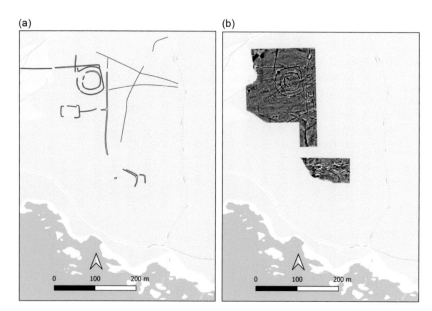

Figure 7 Talland Barton, Cornwall: (a) blue lines indicate potential archaeological features based on aerial survey (data from Cornwall and Isles of Scilly Mapping Project (2020), used under Open Government License v3.0); (b) magnetometry survey superimposed showing the extent and location of subsurface features. © South East Kernow Archaeological Survey (SEKAS). Basemap: OpenStreetMap under the Open Database License (www .openstreetmap.org/copyright).

proved to be Romano-British (dating likely to the first few centuries CE), the field system turned out to be Iron Age and predated the later settlement on the site. It appears that the field system was intentionally filled in and used as part of the foundation of the outer wall for the enclosure, a shift in occupation that the excavators link to the arrival of the Roman military in the region during the first century CE.[36]

2 Telling Stories about Things

Aside from excavation, the study of artefacts is fundamental to archaeological practice. This includes their style and aesthetics (how they look and are decorated); their age and associations (what other material they are found with, on which types of site from which period or periods); their function (what they are used for and by whom); their technology (how they are made, from what materials, using what other objects or practices, and with what gestures); and their meaning (how they were understood by past people, how they were valued,

---

[36] Frieman and Lewis (2022).

what sorts of social practices employed them, what symbolic worlds they engaged with). As with most other domains of archaeological research, even as we develop new analytical methods for studying archaeological artefacts, older techniques continue to be refined and used as our materials and research questions necessitate. So, alongside innovative scientific methods, we must also consider more traditional approaches to material culture.

In the seventeenth and eighteenth centuries, many middle- and upper-class people (mostly men, although not universally) began to develop an interest in the things past people made and used.[37] These *antiquaries* read Greek and Latin texts as well as the Bible and cultivated a studious interest in the natural world and ancient history. They were collectors driven by an interest in possessing (and displaying) unique or unusual items; thus, most artefacts as we know them today were not of interest, and only the complete, decorated, identifiable, and nicest looking were kept. The antiquarian fascination with exotic and ancient things – ancient and ethnographic artefacts as well as elements of the natural environment – underlies the emergence of collecting institutions and material culture studies, both foundational to archaeological practice.[38]

By the middle of the nineteenth century, we see the emergence of archaeology as a discipline, distinct from the (sometimes indiscriminate) collecting practices of individual antiquarians. However, in line with antiquarian interests, early archaeologists expended considerable effort to create structure in the disordered mess of the past. They did so by inventing methodologies to cluster material into coherent geographical and chronological units that could be studied as an assemblage. *Typologies*, the clustering of objects into groups whose members share a specific set of features, are among the oldest and most useful methods of archaeological analysis. For example, in the early nineteenth century, Jens Jacob Asmussen Worsaae used careful observation of the associations between object types and raw materials in *stratified contexts* (i.e., different and discrete stratigraphic layers) to delineate three sequential technological stages in prehistoric Europe (i.e., Europe during the period for which there is no written history): one where only stone-working was practised, one where bronze-working was widespread, and one where iron-working predominated.[39] Other, more ephemeral, technologies, such as weaving, basketry, cooking, and carpentry, were not included. This so-called three-age system is a gross *typo-chronology* in that it gives chronological structure to a sequence of (in this case, quite broad) types of objects.

Most typologies are *formal typologies* (typologies based on the morphology of the objects) that separate objects into groups based on observed or measured

---

[37] Schnapp (1996); Woolf (1997, 2003: 141–82).   [38] Miller (2017: 173–97).
[39] Worsaae (1849).

differences in morphology. This may include decorative patterns, surface texture, various observations about shape, and metric data, such as length, width, curvature, height, weight, and more. Today, metric data are often subject to statistical analysis to help define type clusters. We also see *functional typologies* (typologies based on the function of the objects), although these are somewhat less common today, as historical inferences about function and microscopically visible traces of *usewear* (literally, the patterns of wear resulting from use) rarely align. Nevertheless, functional observations can be integrated into formal typologies to help detail fine distinctions between groups of objects.

Typologies are frequently constructed with chronological questions in mind (see the box 'The Power of Relative Chronologies'); although, before modern scientific dating techniques were invented, if stratigraphic data were not available, chronologies were often inferred based on other archaeological or theoretical elements. In the late 1890s, the British Egyptologist Sir Flinders Petrie excavated hundreds of graves in several cemeteries near the Nile in Upper Egypt at Hu and Abadiyeh, now in the Qena governorate. The graves dated to the predynastic period, meaning there was no available written material to date them; and they included many different types of objects in many different, partially overlapping combinations, including large numbers of decorated ceramics. To effect some sort of chronological order, Petrie developed a method he termed 'sequence dating' (now, more commonly *seriation*).[40] He divided the ceramics into nine classes and then into more than 700 types. He recorded which types were in each of the hundreds of graves and then ordered related assemblages of pottery with regard to each other. His sequence was based on the then current evolutionary principle of gradual, progressive change, meaning he expected to see slow but even changes in practice and form over time. A comparison of this seriation-based relative chronology with radiocarbon chronologies suggests that, while the major structural blocks are correctly ordered, at the smaller scale it is less accurate because his evolutionary framework was too simple.[41]

Archaeologists continue to develop and use typologies and seriation as tools to investigate a range of other questions beyond processes of change over time or the geography of shared cultural practices. In the mid-twentieth century, James Deetz and Edwin Dethlefsen produced a foundational case study of how seriation can give us insights into social practices – in this case, the religious beliefs of New Englanders in the seventeenth through nineteenth centuries.[42] They looked at the changes in ornamentation on colonial New England tombstones (eminently datable objects) and attempted to link the changing styles – from death's heads to more bucolic scenes – to known changes in religious

---

[40] Petrie (1899).   [41] Dee et al. (2014).   [42] Dethlefsen and Deetz (1966).

belief and society. They succeeded in demonstrating not only the way that iconography changed over time (e.g., the obvious death's heads becoming much more abstracted) but also how different fashions in gravestone decoration phased in and out of favour in ways that were meaningfully linked to belief systems and wider religious and social trends (Figure 8). The death's head

Figure 8 Examples of colonial gravestones from cemeteries in Massachusetts, USA. Photographs by Alyne Ricker (top and centre left), Joanne Maynard (centre right, bottom left), and Julie Pritchard (top and bottom right), reproduced with their permission.

design, dating to the seventeenth century, represents a more orthodox, puritanical Christianity stressing decay and death. It was replaced in the eighteenth century by 'winged cherubs', which served as symbols of resurrection and heavenly rewards, a key feature of the Great Awakening, an important religious revival movement of that era. Towards the end of the eighteenth century, willow trees and urns came into use. These were symbols of commemoration and reflected a more secular perspective on death and dying.

The wealth of numeric dating techniques that now abound has challenged chronological sequences based purely on artefact classification, and improvements to excavation methods and scientific analysis have changed our understanding of some types of objects. Today, we are more reflective when we cluster artefacts, recognising that these groupings are largely determined by archaeologists, rather than a reality intrinsic to the things themselves. So, different research questions or clustering methods may well result in different classes or types; and these may not (and likely will not) line up with the classification that the people who originally made and used the objects in question would recognise. The anthropologist Daniel Miller proved this quite definitively in the 1980s with a now classic comparison of an archaeological typology of a contemporary South Asian community's ceramics and that community's own classification of the same ceramic assemblage. The two typologies were entirely distinct, with the formal archaeological classification offering no insight into the community's understanding of the cultural and cosmological significance of their pottery (see the box 'Co-creating Knowledge with Indigenous Communities').[43]

CO-CREATING KNOWLEDGE WITH INDIGENOUS COMMUNITIES

Archaeologists are not the only experts on the past and certainly not always best placed to interpret past artefacts and other material culture. Especially when working with descendant and Indigenous communities, it is important to listen to and incorporate elements of the community's own telling of history because this is the most salient version of their past that exists. Many Indigenous people find the term 'prehistory' to be offensive when applied to their pasts, since it devalues oral and received traditions as well as their connections to their ancestors' practices and ways of life.[44] Although there is no reason oral tradition and archaeological data should agree with each other, sometimes bringing the two together can provide new insights and interpretations.[45]

---

[43] Miller (1985).   [44] Rizvi (2013).   [45] Beck and Somerville (2005).

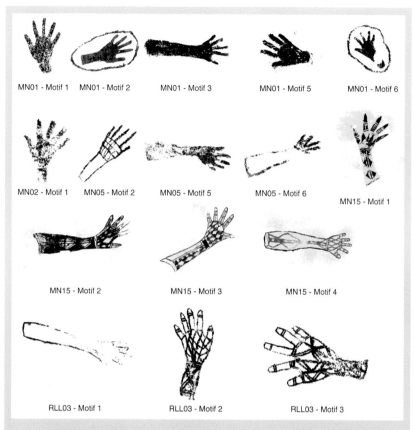

MN01 - Motif 1	MN01 - Motif 2	MN01 - Motif 3	MN01 - Motif 5	MN01 - Motif 6
MN02 - Motif 1	MN05 - Motif 2	MN05 - Motif 5	MN05 - Motif 6	MN15 - Motif 1
MN15 - Motif 2		MN15 - Motif 3	MN15 - Motif 4	
RLL03 - Motif 1		RLL03 - Motif 2	RLL03 - Motif 3	

Figure 9 Digital tracings of some of the Painted Hands from Minjnymirnjdawabu (May et al. 2020, fig. 2).

For example, recent years have seen an explosion of research co-created by Indigenous Australian people and archaeologists to interpret and explain the beautiful and complex art Aboriginal people produced around the continent.[46] Co-creation means that both the archaeologists and Indigenous descendants of the people who originally made the art under study have an equal role in offering interpretations and shaping the final outputs – both scholarly and public. This sort of collaboration allows both archaeologists and communities to find value and meaning in archaeological materials and for the wider community to benefit from new ways to understand the production and significance of Aboriginal art.

For example, the archaeologists Sally K. May and Joakim Goldhahn have worked closely with their Indigenous collaborators to record,

---

[46] For example, O'Connor, Balme, Frederick, et al. (2022); O'Connor, Balme, Oscar, et al. (2022).

analyse, and interpret twentieth-century rock art in northern Australia. The articles they co-author with their Indigenous colleagues reinterpret motifs archaeologists have puzzled to understand, like the hand stencils found across Arnhem Land (Northern Territory) (Figure 9). While some archaeologists suggested they might be drawings of European gloves, May and colleagues argue instead that they represent elements of a particularly important ceremony that formed part of the local Indigenous response to colonial violence and disruption.[47] Indeed, this established collaboration has also begun to provide insights into the lives and practices of specific artists who painted particular places and the sequence and significance of those painting events.[48] The result is a much richer and more nuanced understanding of the production of rock art in the region, told at the scale of the person and their lifespan, rather than the more generalising approach typically taken by archaeologists, who (by necessity) tend to synthesise data across large regions. Moreover, it is written with the aim of benefitting the local Indigenous community, not just other archaeologists.

For early archaeologists, typology demonstrated that it was possible to find order in the archaeological record, and they used newly developed evolutionary models of human society and how change happens to interpret their findings. These do not just inform how archaeologists thought about time but also how they thought about space. The evolutionary models they applied were articulated by anthropologists trying to make sense of different cultural practices between Europeans and the people they were actively colonising. These models delineated narratives of progress from (in one example) stages of savagery and barbarism to civilisation, drawing on social practices like kinship and technologies like agriculture to explain what the scholars involved saw as the superiority of European culture.[49] Nationalist trends within Europe also contributed to a scholarly imperative to study and report national pasts that connected contemporary ethnolinguistic groups to their specific histories and the evolution of their cultures.[50]

Archaeologists brought to this intellectual climate the idea that specific types of objects associated with historically known ethnic groups could be traced to earlier, non-literate periods by typological principles, with less developed versions of more recent objects indicating ancestral cultural connections. In archaeology, the term *culture* carries with it two different concepts. First, an *archaeological culture* represents a body of objects (and associated practices,

---

[47] May et al. (2020).
[48] Goldhahn et al. (2021); Goldhahn et al. (2020); May, Goldhahn et al. (2021); May et al. (2019).
[49] Frieman (2023). [50] Díaz-Andreu García (2007).

deposition locales, buildings, etc.) that are (as an assemblage) unique and geographically bounded; and, second, it implies that that body of objects is distinct in time and recognisably homogeneous. As more and more excavations were carried out, maps of object types yielded regional patterns concerning which specific objects were deposited where. These maps served as the basis for the naming of myriad archaeological cultures and, concomitantly, the emergence of *culture history* in archaeological practice. Archaeological culture-historians were concerned with identifying these cultures, tracing their spread over time, and noting any changes that appear. In a culture-historical perspective, human societies are conservative in that they do not change readily; so, innovations in artefact style, practice, way of life, and so on are thought to result either from diffusion or through the invasion or migration of groups of other people.

Culture-historical approaches dominated how archaeologists studied material culture into the mid-twentieth century, with both positive and negative results. The German archaeologist and philologist Gustaf Kossinna, building on work by linguistic historians and working in an explicitly nationalist and racist framework, used culture history to craft an argument about the origins and superiority of specific Germanic groups.[51] His work was fundamental to many racist interpretations of the past, most notoriously Nazi histories, and inspired considerable investment in archaeology by the Nazi regime.[52] However, when the Australian archaeologist V. Gordon Childe introduced the concept of archaeological cultures into anglophone scholarship in the early twentieth century, he elided many of the uglier racist implications. Instead, over a number of books based on the painstaking study of thousands of prehistoric objects in museum collections across central Europe, Childe used culture history as a framework to construct a new synthesis of European prehistory.[53] His work also engaged closely with shifting ideas of cultural evolution, particularly through a Marxist lens, as well as the contemporary politics of Europe and the wider world. He was widely read by the public, and his impact has been felt well beyond the small world of archaeological researchers.[54]

Evolutionary thinking underpinned both early chronologies and later culture histories, and (in more complex forms) it continues to play a significant role in the archaeological interpretation of technological and social change. While nineteenth- and early twentieth-century concepts of evolution tended to be unilineal and progressive (change happens in one way and one direction), the burgeoning archaeological evidence made clear this was too simple a model. The middle of the twentieth century saw an effort by North American cultural

---

[51] Kossinna (1928).   [52] Arnold (1990).   [53] Childe (1925, 1929, 1934).   [54] Irving (2020).

anthropologists, including Leslie White and Julian Steward, to revive evolutionary models by giving them a more scientific basis.[55] Their work was founded on empirical evidence from areas of archaeology, palaeontology, and historiography and embodied an attempt at developing a new descriptive and objective scientific model of cultural evolution. They discarded the concept of progress (and moral judgements regarding more or less evolved societies) and directionality (i.e., that social development went in only one direction) and embraced multilineal explanations of change. This framework underlay the scientific turn archaeology took in the mid-twentieth century (the emergence of the so-called *New Archaeology* or *processual archaeology*); and evolutionary modelling – often closely allied with computational methods and more closely linked to biological approaches – remains an influential approach to the study of archaeological technologies, now thankfully shorn of the assumptions of earlier generations (see the box 'Evolutionary Models of Stone Tool Technology').

EVOLUTIONARY MODELS OF STONE TOOL TECHNOLOGY

The evolutionary turn of the late twentieth century has had a profound impact on some scientific archaeologists. Building on foundational work by evolutionary biologists,[56] archaeologists and anthropologists began to develop models of transmission and change over time that were based in the idea that social practices and technological systems are subject to similar evolutionary pressures as organisms.[57] In recent years, archaeologists have developed sophisticated micro- and macroevolutionary approaches to interrogate a range of cultural practices, from potting styles to the spread of iron-working recipes, to long-term continuity, to the links between cognitive evolution and changing stone tool technologies.[58] Although sometimes quite methodologically complex and rather varied in detail and theoretical outlook, these approaches have the potential to open up new analytical inroads, allowing novel ideas or interpretations of well-known material to be developed.

For example, the Brazilian archaeologists Mercedes Okumura and Astolfo Araujo set out to develop a new interpretation of so-called Umbu Tradition stemmed points – knapped stone tools found over a wide area in Uruguay, Argentina, and Brazil that seemed to have been produced for more than 10,000 years by local hunter-gatherers.[59] This long period of use and

---

[55] Steward (1955); White (1959).   [56] Dawkins (1976); Wilson (1975).
[57] Boyd and Richerson (1985); Dunnell (1980).
[58] Kuhn (2020); O'Brien and Shennan (2010); Prentiss (2019).
[59] Okumura and Araujo (2014).

extremely large geographic distribution do not fit traditional models of distinct types of artefacts with clear cultural and temporal associations. In an attempt to identify formal differences among the stemmed points from the site of Garivaldino in southern Brazil that could indicate change over time at this site, they used traditional and computational methods to identify similarities and differences in shape, analysed raw materials, and compared their results to the site's radiocarbon sequence. They found considerable variation but no change over time. Instead, they argue that the lack of change is itself indicative of social and environmental conditions. They apply an evolutionary model that suggests innovations emerge from demographic pressure, so the small population and stable environmental conditions experienced during the Holocene in this region could, in fact, have allowed long-standing traditions to flourish. They make the point that this was not a passive process but an active cultural mechanism, indicating a strongly conformist value system.

New scientific methods and technical advances in materials analysis and microscopy have opened new horizons for our understanding of objects. We can directly date objects that previously we could only sequence. We are able to study the microscopic traces left by manufacturing and use processes to reconstruct the gestures and techniques past people used in their daily lives. We have myriad tools to study raw materials, giving us insights into the movement of objects, changing technologies, and how these were shaped or themselves shaped social and political structures (see the box 'Determining the Prehistoric Diet from Northeast Asian Ceramics'). Within the broad subfield of *ethnoarchaeology*, some archaeologists work with contemporary artisans and practitioners of traditional technologies to draw insights about archaeological material. For example, Maria-Louise Sideroff conducted ethnographic research at the Zizia pottery factory (Jordan) to understand the social and technological organisation of first-millennium-CE pottery workshops in this region.[60] Moreover, largely following approaches developed by French sociologists and archaeologists, we have developed a methodological toolkit to reconstruct various *chaînes opératoires* (occasionally translated as 'operational sequences' but usually retained in French), that is, the sequences of techniques (including gestures) and processes past people employed to make, use, and rework objects prior to their eventual discard.[61] This technological approach to material culture

---

[60] Sidoroff (2015).

[61] Lemonnier (1992); Leroi-Gourhan (1964); Pelegrin (1990); Schlanger (1994).

is complemented by an interpretative framework drawing attention to the life history or biography of objects.[62] In this way, the technological approach treats things as dynamic and the material form identified by archaeologists upon discovery as just one phase in what may have been an extended period of use and circulation.

DETERMINING THE PREHISTORIC DIET FROM NORTHEAST ASIAN CERAMICS

Ceramics are among the most intensively studied artefacts in archaeological assemblages because they tend to be well-preserved and can offer us considerable information into the economic, social, and environmental elements of past people's lives. Sophisticated macroscopic and microscopic methods of ceramic analysis have been developed, including typological and stylistic study of pottery forms and decorative patterns, experimental reproduction to determine production sequences, thin-section microscopy and portable X-ray fluorescence analysis (pXRF) to identify the raw materials chosen for the *fabric* (i.e., the mix of clay or paste and temper), and residue analysis to distinguish the traces of food cooked in a given pot.[63]

Although pottery production and use are often linked to the adoption of agriculture, settled communities, and other 'Neolithic' ways of life, it is sometimes also used by people living hunter-gatherer lifestyles. This was the case in East Asia (southern China, Japan, and the Russian Far East) from at least 16,000 years ago – millennia before agriculture came to the region. The Japanese archaeologist Shinya Shoda and his colleagues have conducted residue analysis to study how people were using this pottery. They found that, in coastal and riverine regions, it was mostly used for processing fish and other aquatic resources, while in inland areas ruminant fats were detected.[64] In Japan, at least, their data suggest thousands of years of association between ceramics and the preparation of aquatic resources, leading them to argue that early pottery was used uniquely for cooking seafood or the fermentation of fish pastes related to prestigious events like public feasting.[65]

As an example, we can look at the changing interpretation of green ground-stone axes from the European Neolithic. These axes date roughly to the sixth to fourth millennium BCE and have been studied typologically for decades.[66] New microscopic analytical techniques, chiefly spectroradiometry, have made clear that a small subset of ground-stone axes (often those with a high polish and no

---

[62] Joy (2009).   [63] Orton and Hughes (2013); Rice (2015).
[64] Lucquin et al. (2018); Shoda et al. (2017); Shoda et al. (2020).
[65] Lucquin et al. (2016); Shoda (2021).   [66] Pétrequin, Cassen, Gauthier et al. (2012).

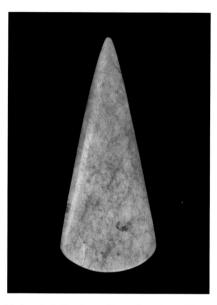

Figure 10 Axe of Alpine jadeite from Greenlawdean, Berwickshire, Scotland. © National Museums Scotland.

damage from having been used: Figure 10) are made from jadeites traceable to only a couple of quite remote sources in the Italian Alps. Although they share a raw material source, these axes take many forms; and technological study makes clear that they are all reworked to local preferences. Many also show evidence of having been highly and repeatedly polished, sometimes to a glassy sheen. Pierre Pétrequin and his research team have argued that the formal variability results in part from specialist manufacture processes (including repolishing) that were part of the ceremonial use and display of these obviously very special axes.[67] In other words, although raw material analysis clusters all alpine axes together, formal analysis groups them differently – and sometimes includes axes of other raw materials based on their shape, function, or deposition location. However, by combining many different analytical techniques (both scientific and traditional) we are able to develop new information about how local communities engaged with supra-regional value systems and exchange networks.

Computational methods have also shifted the sorts of questions we can ask of objects and the quantities and complexity of data we can analyse about them. Archaeological computing has been an increasingly important part of the field since the 1970s, with early applications including polythetic classifications of

---

[67] Pétrequin, Cassen, Errera et al. (2012).

artefacts through statistical clustering, a method called *numerical taxonomy* by
the British archaeologist David Clarke who applied it to developing a new
typology of late third-millennium-BCE pottery.[68] In recent years, network
analysis has been widely adopted by computational archaeologists to study a
range of questions. For example, Barbara Mills and colleagues have combined
data on raw material sources used for obsidian tools and established formal
typologies of precolonial ceramics from the American Southwest and applied
social network analysis (SNA) to explore patterns of connection and affiliation
between communities. Building outwards from the artefacts, they explore
patterns of innovation adoption and are able to identify a fragmentation in
social networks after 1300 CE as well as patterns of affiliation between communities that they have linked to the movement of ceramic-making marriage
partners.[69]

The last two decades have seen a renewed interest in artefacts both in
archaeology and more widely in the social sciences and humanities. This so-
called material turn has focussed attention on the complex ways people engage
with objects and their tangible materiality.[70] Following this body of research,
objects are not just passive reflections of human practices and beliefs. Instead,
they mediate our relationships with other people, are entangled in our sense of
self, and are fundamental to how we navigate the world around us (Figure 11).[71]
The significance to archaeology of these concepts is that, in studying material
culture, its movements, and its raw materials, we are effectively looking at the
material remains of people's selves and of their relationships. The choices they
made about the things they manufactured and used reflect their own views of
how they were related to other people and to these specific types of material
culture.[72] Additionally, there has been an increasing interest in the emotive
quality of the archaeological record. This forms part of the larger material turn
in that it attempts to capture the intangible, emotional impact of past materialities and bring that into our archaeological narratives.

For example, the Australian archaeologist Bettina Liebelt has proposed a new
approach to understanding the value and meaning of grinding stones (non-
portable Aboriginal stone tools used to grind grain or to sharpen axes).[73] She
tacks back and forth among a variety of very different emotional experiences of
their materiality from her own experience as an archaeologist encountering
these objects in collections and *in situ* in the landscape, to that of white farmers
who recover grinding stones on their property and often assemble large personal
collections, to that of the Indigenous descendants of the people who made and

[68] Clarke (1970).   [69] Mills (2018); Mills et al. (2016); Mills et al. (2013).
[70] Bennett (2010); Miller (2005).   [71] Dobres (2000); Hicks (2010).   [72] Hodder (2012).
[73] Liebelt (2019).

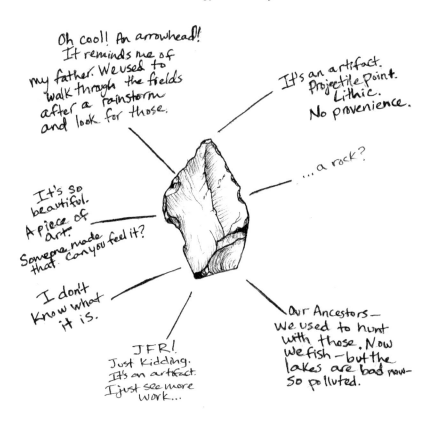

Figure 11 'Interprets' illustrating the many ways we interpret even the humblest stone tool. © Beth Compton.

used them. Her goal here is to develop a more expansive approach to lithic analysis that invites in and builds from the experiences of her collaborators, especially her Indigenous collaborators, while also allowing a diversity of perspectives and interpretations to coexist alongside her own archaeological analysis. In this way, she is able to contextualise her scientific work to enrich our understanding of the ways these grindstones formed part of past technological systems and how they continue to be active parts of relationships between people, their ancestors, and the land they occupy, care for, and farm.

3 Telling Stories about Time

'How old is that?' is not just one of the first questions a member of the public is likely to ask an archaeologist but also one of the key preoccupations of the field of archaeology itself. Dating and sequencing the relics of past people's lives have been part of the study of the archaeological record since before the discipline emerged. Antiquarians and early archaeologists used written accounts – primarily classical texts and the Bible – to make sense of ancient monuments and archaeological artefacts. Since the middle of the twentieth century, scientific methods of dating specific types of materials have also been developed, often providing greater precision and accuracy to the practice of archaeological dating (though not always). Determining the ages of archaeological sites and materials is important because it both lets us order the archaeological record chronologically and gives us insights into the process, speed, and geography of changes in practice, technology, and society over time.

Many early antiquarians were devoutly Christian and struggled to imagine – or even rejected in principle the idea of – a world or sequence of events that did not accord with the Christian Bible.[74] Even those less worried about heresy tended to think within a biblical framework, so the generations of descent from Adam and Eve provided the chronological scope in which all past events must have taken place, and anomalous finds – such as the fossilised bones of ancient megafauna and dinosaurs – were hypothesised as evidence for the biblical flood or as proof that, as humans became more sinful over time, the stature of people (and other fauna, one presumes) shrank accordingly.[75] Classical literature provided other interpretative frameworks, but these often relied on a mix of historical information in texts and mythical narratives about the past as recorded by ancient authors. Allegorical narratives of past ages detailed in classical texts – a golden age followed by the increasingly dissolute silver age, bronze age, and, finally, iron age – shaped the antiquarian imaginary.[76] Our present rough divisions of Stone Age, Bronze Age, and Iron Age emerge directly from that source of inspiration.

Written and oral histories can be extremely useful for dating archaeological sites and contexts. Dates in lists of kings, on funerary monuments, and on coins obviously offer extremely valuable information about the dates of a specific archaeological context, layer, or group of associated materials. Coins in particular can be very useful for establishing a *terminus post quem* or *terminus ante quem* (literally 'end after which' or 'end before which') for associated archaeological contexts. For example, in 1938 Alexander Keillor excavated a skeleton from beneath a fallen standing stone in the famous Avebury henge and standing stone arrangement in south-west England. Accompanying the individual were a

---

[74] Trigger (2006: 118–20).   [75] Piggott (1989: 48–52).   [76] Schnapp (1996).

pair of scissors, a buckle, a wooden-handled probe, and three silver coins datable to 1320–50 CE (with the earlier part of the range more likely).[77] The coins provide us a *terminus post quem* of 1320 for this burial: for them to have been found with the buried individual, they must have already been in circulation at the time of the burial, hence the burial cannot have occurred prior to 1320. This is significant, because other finds from the pit in which the individual was recovered include sherds of late twelfth- and early thirteenth-century-CE ceramics, which, in the absence of the coins, might have incorrectly dated the burial 150 years too early. Because of the coins, we can understand the sherds to be residual in the soil, that is, broken bits of old rubbish that were already in the soil in the early fourteenth century and became incorporated into the burial when the hole was dug and then refilled.

Similarly, oral narratives can help us understand sequences of activity at sites with no written records but abundant local memories. The rhythms of oral history and the archaeological record often exist at angles to each other: the sense of timing and tempo within a personal memory or preserved narrative rarely accords with linear calendrical time or archaeological dates, and the historical element prized by archaeologists is often tangential to much more significant focus on cultural practice, kin relations, legal doctrine, spiritual concerns, and more.[78] Nevertheless, both when they accord and when they diverge, oral histories enrich archaeological narratives and give new significance to archaeological data that are otherwise inexplicable. For example, McKechnie compared Nuu-chah-nulth oral traditions about occupation of settlement sites in the Broken Group archipelago (British Columbia, Canada) with radiocarbon dates from the excavation of these settlements.[79] Both the oral traditions and the radiometric dating offered the same sequence of construction and occupation for these sites; but the oral traditions also indicate the connections between specific sites, creating separate lineages of settlement sites, providing social and political context for their foundation and use, and drawing out patterns of relation that span from at least 1,800 years ago to the present. Similarly, the anthropologist and historian Chris Ballard describes how chiefly genealogies in Vanuatu and Tonga create a historical sequence that incorporates social lineage, important historical individuals and events, and patterns of occupation and mobility that can be distinguished archaeologically.[80]

At a very basic level, there are two sorts of archaeological dates: *relative dates* and *numerical dates* (sometimes called *absolute dates*). Relative dating methods provide us with information about the sequence of archaeological sites

---

[77] Gillings et al. (2008: 277–8).   [78] Jones and Russell (2012).   [79] McKechnie (2015).
[80] Ballard (2016, 2020).

and artefacts (which is older, which is more recent), without giving us a calendrical date for those sites and artefacts. The principle of *stratigraphy* and the construction of typologies (as discussed in Section 1) underlie many relative chronologies (see the box 'The Power of Relative Chronologies'). There are a variety of methods of numerical dating available to archaeologists today, depending on the material they are studying, the antiquity of this material, the local environment in which the material was deposited, and their budget.[81] Broadly, we can talk about five different types of dating techniques: radiometric dating, chemical alteration dating, magnetism dating, trapped charge dating, and layer counting. Some of these methods can be and are regularly combined, others are used for specific periods or materials. The older and more established a method, the better we understand its pros and cons, so established methods like radiocarbon dating and dendrochronology are more common than newer more complex approaches like archaeomagnetic dating or optically stimulated luminescence. The choice of methods also depends on variables such as the level of precision necessary, the materials available for dating, the period to be dated, and the cost of analysis. Table 2 gives a brief overview of some major methods, the materials and periods they are used to date, and the specific thing they measure. This table is not comprehensive; new dating techniques are constantly being invented and existing methods are continually being improved, since numerical dating is such a core part of archaeological science. This section will expand on a few of these.

THE POWER OF RELATIVE CHRONOLOGIES

Relative dating methods can be very powerful when combined with careful observation and good archaeological practice. One of the first and most robust demonstrations of this power comes from Scandinavia. Oscar Montelius was an archaeologist employed by the Swedish Museum of National Antiquities from 1968. Inspired by the work of earlier Danish archaeologists Christian Jürgensen Thomsen and Jens Jacob Asmussen Worsaae, he aimed to develop a chronological sequence for Swedish prehistory and to assign calendrical dates to the period, but he had no local written evidence and numeric dating had not yet been invented.[82]

To solve this problem, Montelius relied on carefully excavated and clearly stratified deposits. He carefully documented artefacts in different stratigraphic layers in *sealed deposits* (archaeological features that have not been disturbed since they formed or were deposited), and he compared these with artefacts from equally well-preserved stratigraphic layers from

---

[81] Rink et al. (2015).   [82] Gräslund (1987); Trigger (2006: 223–30).

Germany and other southern regions.[83] This process combined strati-graphic sequences with detailed typological observation. His basic assumption was that if Sword Type A from Sweden and Sword Type B from Germany were very similar then they likely formed part of the same chronological horizon, as would all the other material culture with which they were each associated in sealed stratigraphic deposits. This process is called *cross-dating*. By meticulously cross-dating artefacts south towards the Mediterranean, Montelius eventually reached the Aegean where he found artefacts in his schema that had themselves been cross-dated around the Mediterranean to literate regions like Egypt. Thus, they were able to be given calendrical dates, linked to Egyptian royal genealogies. Montelius used his cross-dated network of object typologies to link those dates with the stratigraphically sequenced Swedish Bronze Age artefacts.

Montelius used this to divide the Swedish Bronze Age into six periods, each about 200 years long and all given calendrical dates based on the Egyptian king lists. His typological sequence has proved extremely robust, and his periods remain firmly in use in southern Scandinavia for identifying and sequencing Bronze Age artefacts. However, when radiocarbon dating was first introduced, his dates were deemed inaccurate. With the realisation that radiocarbon dates needed to be calibrated (see the box 'Why and How Do We Calibrate Radiocarbon Dates?'), his work was re-evaluated; and, in a testament to the care and attention to detail with which he approached his research, his dating was more or less vindicated.[84] Although the radiometric dates are not identical to the ones Montelius deduced, they only differ from his by a few decades, an extraordinary result.

Radiocarbon dating is probably the best-known numerical dating method that archaeologists use and one of the most widely practised isotopic dating methods. The element carbon forms part of all living and once-living organisms on earth, and several different isotopes of carbon exist. The stable isotopes of carbon are ^{12}C and ^{13}C, but ^{14}C is radioactive (hence, 'radiocarbon'), decaying over time into ^{14}N, which is stable. Most ^{14}C is formed in the upper atmosphere when ^{14}N absorbs neutrons which are themselves the product of a cascade of reactions caused by cosmic rays. This ^{14}C is rapidly oxidised to CO_2 which is incorporated into the biosphere through photosynthesis. ^{14}C's rate of decay, its *half-life*, is uniform: it takes 5,730 years for 50 per cent of the ^{14}C present to decay to ^{14}N,

---

[83] Montelius (1903, 1986).   [84] Hornstrup et al. (2012); Vandkilde et al. (1996).

Table 2 Some major methods of numeric dating.

Dating technique type	Name	Specific thing measured	Typical material analysed	Suitable date range	Precision
Radiometric dating techniques	Radiocarbon; C14	Carbon isotopes (ratio of $^{14}C/^{13}C$)	Charcoal, bone, shell, plant parts	50,000 years ago to present	100s to 1000s of years (after calibration)
	Uranium series; U-series (includes Uranium-Thorium; U-Th; Thorium-230; Th-230)	Uranium and daughter isotopes (ratio of $^{238}U/^{234}U/^{230}Th$)	Tooth enamel, maybe bone, speleothem (accretions of mineral deposits in caves), coral	600,000 years ago to a few years ago	Really complicated and only provides a minimum age; uncertainty rate is <1 per cent of estimated age for speleothem and coral, much higher for bone
	Argon-Argon; Ar-Ar	Argon isotopes (ratio of $^{40}Ar/^{39}Ar$)	Igneous or volcanic deposits	4 billion to 1,000 years ago	100s to 100,000s of years
Chemical alteration dating techniques	Amino acid racemisation; AAR	The extent of post-mortem conversion of biological forms of amino acids to non-biological forms	Shell, eggshell, maybe tooth enamel	>150,000 years to present	10s to 1000s of years but dependent on quality of calibration curve and material used

Trapped charge methods	Optically stimulated luminescence; OSL	The energy required to free an electron trapped since last exposure to light	Quartz grains in sediment	200,000 years ago to present	Uncertainty rate of about 5 per cent of estimated age
	Electron spin resonance; ESR	The energy required to change the spin of an unpaired electron	Tooth enamel, coral, shell, speleothem, silicate sediments	Usually 600,000 to <20,000 years ago, but can be used from 2–3 million years ago if conditions are right	Uncertainty rate of about 5 per cent of estimated age
Layer counting	Dendrochronology	Wood with annual growth rings	Charcoal, core from wooden artefact or architectural element	c.12,000 years ago to present (depending on location)	<1 year
	Tephrochronology	Tephra (microscopic volcanic particles)	Layers or deposits above or below a tephra horizon	4 billion years ago to present (in combination with another dating technique)	Variable: from <1 year to wider range depending on dating method and the number of layers counted
	Ice core dating	Seasonal depositions of dust and sea salt, isochrons, seasonal isotopic signatures of water in continuously forming glacial ice deposits	Sequential layers in continuous cores of deep ice	c.700,000 years ago to present (depending on location)	Variable: from <1 year to wider range depending on dating method

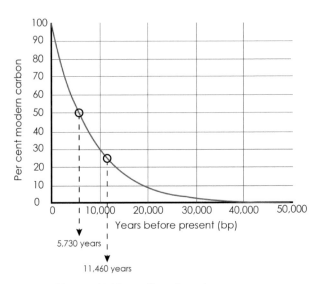

Figure 12 The radiocarbon decay curve.

allowing scientists to model it on a regular decay curve (Figure 12). During an organism's life, it assimilates ^{14}C from carbon dioxide; but, upon its death, it stops exchanging carbon with the biosphere and the ^{14}C content begins to decrease following the decay curve. The presence of ^{14}C in organic material and its regular decay were first proposed by the American scientist Willard Libby.[85] Archaeologists were engaged with his work from the start, and he was awarded the Nobel Prize in Chemistry in 1960 for this discovery.[86] Following Libby's approach, we measure the proportion of ^{14}C to ^{12}C in an organic sample, such as bone or charcoal, in order to estimate its age. Since the proportion of ^{14}C in the atmosphere varies with, for example, fluctuations in cosmic rays hitting the upper atmosphere, we need to calibrate the radiocarbon determinations to calculate a calendar age estimate (see the box 'Why and How Do We Calibrate Radiocarbon Dates?'). Archaeologists distinguish between the uncalibrated radiocarbon date and the calibrated date using the units bp ('before present', i.e., 1950) and cal BP (or cal BCE/CE) where 'cal' means calibrated, although the notation has changed over time and some care is needed to assess which timescale is being reported. Because of its relatively short half-life, radiocarbon is only useful for dating material from the last c.50,000 years.

WHY AND HOW DO WE CALIBRATE RADIOCARBON DATES?

Early applications of radiocarbon dating assumed that the ^{14}C/^{12}C ratio in the atmosphere was fixed, but this is not the case (Figure 13). Discrepancies between the dates of objects and written sources provoked

[85] Libby (1946).   [86] Taylor (1985).

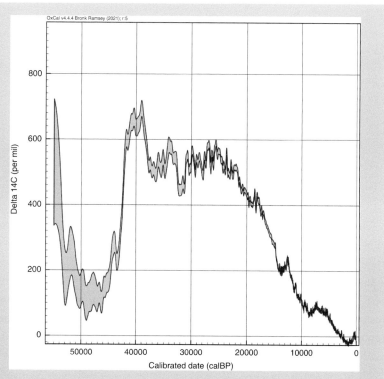

OxCal v4.4.4 Bronk Ramsey (2021); r:5

Figure 13 Curve showing the change in ('delta') C^{14} in the atmosphere from c.55,000 years ago to the present, based on the northern hemisphere data exported from OxCal (data from Reimer et al. 2020).

considerable research to determine whether a model of atmospheric carbon could be developed so that the radiocarbon measurements in labs could be calibrated to calendar years.

In order to get sequential data on changing atmospheric carbon ratios, scientists turned to tree rings which form annually, preserving a record of environmental conditions from one year to the next. Careful observation and analysis of long-lived tree species led to the development of the first radiocarbon calibration curve, which showed details of long- and short-term fluctuations in atmospheric carbon ratios extending thousands of years into the past.[87] Tree ring data, in the form of established *dendrochronologies*, continue to be used to calibrate radiocarbon dates, alongside other sequences, including coral, varves, foraminifera, and speleothems. Due to a greater maritime influence from the larger expanse of oceans in the southern hemisphere, organisms in the southern hemisphere assimilate

---

[87] Stuiver and Suess (1966).

different amounts of radiocarbon to organisms in the northern hemisphere, so separate calibration curves have had to be developed for the northern and southern hemispheres.[88] As these calibration curves fluctuate, dates are not points in time but probability curves that can be modelled using a range of statistical approaches (see the box 'More Probable Than Absolute').

A variety of software is freely available to calibrate and model raw radiocarbon data. The major online calibration programs are Calib, Calpal, and OxCal. RCarbon is a calibration and modelling package for the statistical program R.[89]

Tephrochronologies are less well known than radiocarbon dating, though scientists have been constructing them since the 1960s, and the field is well-established.[90] They have the advantage that they can provide dates for deposits of any age, as long as a tephra layer is present and has been identified with a specific volcanic event. Tephra is a mix of volcanic ash, rock, and minerals ejected from volcanoes during eruption. A tephra plume from a large volcanic eruption can travel thousands of kilometres on the wind after an eruption, eventually falling to the ground and forming tephra deposits. These may be visible to the naked eye or require lengthy chemical protocols and microscopic investigations to find in a sedimentary layer. Following Lane and colleagues, many tephra deposits are chemically distinct because of processes occurring within the magma chamber.[91] Careful analysis of the chemical composition of the tephra can 'fingerprint' a given deposit, allowing it to be linked back to its source volcanic eruption. Since a tephra layer derives from a single volcanic eruption and is simultaneously deposited after that eruption, once identified it can be considered an *isochron* (an event that occurs simultaneously). This provides a powerful tool to precisely link archaeological sites and palaeoenvironmental records. In many cases, the tephra layer can also provide a numerical age estimate, as tephra can be directly dated using Ar/Ar. It can also be dated by a range of methods when found within a sequence. For example, tephra found in an ice core can be precisely dated by layer counting, and the age of tephra found in lake sequences can be estimated by radiocarbon dating plant material in sediments above and below the tephra. This age can then be transferred to any deposit in which the tephra is found.

[88] Hogg et al. (2020); Reimer et al. (2020).
[89] Calib (http://intcal.qub.ac.uk/calib/), Calpal (www.calpal.de/), OxCal (http://c14.arch.ox.ac.uk/embed.php?File=oxcal.html), RCarbon (https://cran.r-project.org/web/packages/rcarbon/index.html).
[90] Lowe et al. (2022).   [91] Lane et al. (2017).

Luminescence dating, particularly optically stimulated luminescence, is commonly applied to Pleistocene-aged archaeology (and increasingly more recent periods where radiocarbon is not available) and most often uses quartz or sand. The underlying science of luminescence techniques is quite complex, but the basic idea is that, over time, ionising radiation from the uranium, thorium, and potassium that are naturally found in sediment will cause electrons to be released within quartz. These electrons can be trapped in defects in the crystalline structure of quartz (the *trapped charge*) and emptied by exposure to light. So, the traps are emptied (or *zeroed*) when a grain of sand is blown into an archaeological site and exposed to light. Once buried, the trapped charge will begin to build up again in proportion to the amount of uranium, potassium, and thorium in the sediment. Because exposure to light would empty the traps, samples must be collected in the dark, usually by inserting a core into a trench's vertical profile, but sometimes with a teaspoon and a red flashlight while tarps block the sun. In the lab, quartz grains are exposed to light, once again emptying the electron traps. When electron traps are emptied, some traps will cause the crystal to glow faintly, or luminesce. By measuring how much the grains luminesce, and the amount of uranium, thorium, and potassium in the sediment, we can determine the total amount of radiation received during burial and the radiation dose per year and so calculate the age since burial. The advantage of this method, especially OSL, is that it can date dirt, that is, the sediment within which archaeological material is found.

At Riwi Cave in Western Australia, Rachel Wood and colleagues combined radiocarbon and OSL dating to date one of the oldest occupied rock shelters in north-west Australia, a key site for understanding human expansion across the continent.[92] As this process of expansion was understood to take place between 30,000 and 50,000 years ago, radiocarbon dating alone would not suffice. For the phases where both OSL and radiocarbon dates were available, they compared the modelled dates and determined that both methods agreed on the sequence and phasing and could be deemed more or less equivalently accurate. The combination of the methods, as well as the large number of samples (forty-four radiocarbon, thirty-seven OSL) with high-precision strati-graphic information, greatly increased the precision of the site's dating, allowing them to suggest an 1,800-year period – 46,000–44,600 cal BP (95.4 per cent probability) – during which the cave was first occupied by people.

Dating the early occupation of Sahul – the large continent that includes Australia, Papua New Guinea, and quite a lot of land now lying beneath the

---
[92] Wood et al. (2016).

Indian Ocean – is a major focus of Australian archaeologists but often of considerably less interest to Indigenous Australians. First Nations people in Australia, as in other parts of the world, have deep personal and cosmological connections to Country, the land they and their people are from and for which they are responsible, and understand themselves as having always been part of their Country.[93] This contrasts with the archaeological story of people arriving in Australia at some point in the past (currently, we think that was sometime between 65,000 and 50,000 years ago).

These two narratives exist in separate temporalities: one governed by numeric dating and one by personal connection and kin relations. For example, the Noongar musician and scholar Clint Bracknell explores how Noongar song builds relations between distant and recent times, incorporating new people, places, plants, and animals, into established networks of relation.[94] This gives the incomer deep roots, tying them into the web of obligation that underpins Noongar people's past and present ties to Country. When we make the effort to speak across these divergent temporalities, our narratives of sequence, lineage, genealogy, and time are enriched.[95] Indeed, the Cree-Métis archaeologist Paulette Steeves brought together First Nations knowledge and archaeological data to argue for a much longer occupation of North America than is traditionally accepted, a controversial but stimulating result.[96]

Moreover, temporality – that is, the flow of time – is not necessarily linear or regular. Although we are habituated to thinking of time in terms of a single calendar of dates that proceed one after the other from past directly to present, time itself – and even calendrical systems – take different forms.[97] For example, the Catholic church (like many other Christian denominations) follows a series of embedded circular (that is, looping) ecclesiastical calendars that advance cyclically: an annual cycle tracking a series of holy days and saints' days through liturgical seasons, as well as cycles of readings and liturgies on separate biennial and triennial cycles. Many different individuals or societies also conceptualise time as passing in cyclical, circular, or other non-linear patterns. Moreover, anthropologists and Indigenous people alike observe that ceremony, song, and dance can collapse temporal distinctions on the individual level, bringing *then* and *now* together into a singular, embodied experience.[98] These temporal regimes may coexist with others, just as European calendrical time coexists with cyclical ecclesiastical calendars, as well as with personal experiences of the numinous that may erase

---

[93] Neale and Kelly (2020).   [94] Bracknell (2023).   [95] McGrath et al. (2023).
[96] Steeves (2021).   [97] Gell (1992); Munn (1992).   [98] Barwick (2023); Gell (1992: 27–9).

any temporal distance between the origin of a sacred text or object and the religionist's spiritual encounter with it.[99]

Even within a purely archaeological context, we are constantly working across multiple temporalities. As Table 2 shows, different numerical dating techniques offer different margins of error that shape our 'absolute' chronologies, and the dates themselves are individual probability curves (see the box 'More Probable Than Absolute'), so they can be modelled to tell a variety of stories, depending on the research questions and prior assumptions. At any one site, we may be speaking across numerical dates with error ranges from tens to thousands of years – that is, from a part of a human life to tens of generations – as well as working with stratigraphic sequences, typological chronologies, and archaeological features that might represent anything from a momentary act (the loss of a tool) to a few hours of activity (a single hearth) to days of occupation (the butchery of a large animal) to years or more (a house, settlement, or ritual site which may well include its own seasonal rhythms). Time is complicated, and so our temporal narratives are too. This complexity is a key source of uncertainty in the archaeological record, but it is also a major locus of inspiration: since our chronologies are multiple rather than singular, we can experiment with them, applying different techniques, models, or data to explore the possibilities of the archaeological record and the sequences of human action it preserves.

MORE PROBABLE THAN ABSOLUTE

When archaeologists report numerical dates in publications, they almost always provide an age range rather than a single year. The range represents the *margin of error* of any given reading and might extend from years to decades to centuries or even millennia depending on the method used, the antiquity of the date, the quality of the sample, and the quality of the analysis. The goal of numerical dating is to be as accurate and precise as necessary to investigate a given phenomenon. The reason precision is important is because the date may fall anywhere within the margin of error quoted. For example, archaeologists normally work within the 95 per cent probability range (or two-sigma). If an age estimate for a seed is in the range 1769–1615 cal BCE at 95 per cent probability, the sample has a 95 per cent chance of having grown between these dates, but also a one in twenty chance of having grown outside of this age range (Figure 14).

While an individual age estimate may help us better sequence an artefact or stratigraphic layer, by itself it offers little further information.

---

[99] Rademaker (2023).

However, since dates are probabilities, not single numbers, there are a variety of statistical modelling techniques that can be applied to do much more with these data, depending on the types of questions we pose. A number of dates from a single site can be modelled together to refine local sequences or model the age of undated phases.[100] There are also a variety of methods to model dates from different sites together to test hypotheses statistically, for example about the timing of a change in technology or the impact of climatic variation.[101] More recently, archaeologists have been exploring whether large assemblages of dates from many sites could be modelled as demographic proxies, indicating phases of population growth or shrinkage.[102]

The commonest form of modelling incorporates archaeological observations into the assessment of date ranges in order to create more precise date ranges. If you have a number of dates from a single site with good stratigraphic or typological control, that is, you understand the stratigraphic or artefact typological sequence well and can assign all your dates to specific stratigraphic phases, then you can build a model that takes this sequence into account using *Bayesian statistical methods* and assumes dates from the oldest layers to be older than dates from the most recent.[103] This should narrow the margin of error for all your dates, increase their precision (sometimes to the scale of a human lifetime), and allow you to model dates for phases where no samples for dating were available. These models are also probabilistic, that is, they have margins of error, and can yield different results depending on what prior assumptions are built in and how.

In one famous application, Alex Bayliss and colleagues modelled thirty dates from the famous prehistoric mound of Silbury Hill in southwest England, a monumental site (it is 40 m high with a base diameter of 160 m) that had been roughly dated to the third millennium BCE.[104] They presented two models, based on slightly different interpretations of the archaeology. In one, the various phases of construction took place over 140–435 years (at 95 per cent probability); in the second, construction took place over 1–115 years (at 95 per cent probability). A subsequent Bayesian model building on their work suggested that the mound was constructed in three phases between the late twenty-fifth and the late twenty-third century BCE, a period likely spanning 55–155 years.[105]

---

[100] Bayliss (2009).   [101] For example, Schauer et al. (2021); Wood et al. (2014).
[102] Bronk Ramsey (2017).   [103] Bronk Ramsey (2009).   [104] Bayliss et al. (2007).
[105] Leary et al. (2013: 111).

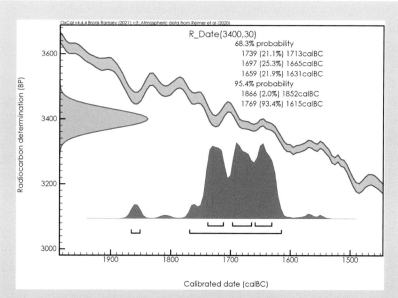

Figure 14 A radiocarbon date calibrated using OxCal
(Bronk Ramsey 2021).

The uncalibrated date (3400 bp) and its margin of error of thirty years are
visualised as a red probability curve on the *y*-axis; the blue line is the IntCal
northern hemisphere radiocarbon calibration curve (Reimer et al. 2020); and the grey
curve on the *x*-axis represents the probability of the calibrated date corresponding
to any given calendrical year given the fluctuations in atmospheric 14C.

Although any type of numerical date can be statistically modelled,
currently these methods are most commonly applied to radiocarbon as
these are the most abundant data available.

4 Telling Stories about People

The real goal of most archaeology is not to dig holes, order objects, or
develop chronologies; it is to understand better the lives, societies, and
worlds of past people.[106] All the stratigraphic analysis, close object study,
and dating methods are part of this process, alongside the application of a
variety of interpretative frameworks. In addition, we sometimes have
access to the physical remains of past people, and these too can be studied
to offer quite granular information about an individual's health, habitual
practices, geographical origins, and genetic lineage. As these data accrue,

---

[106] Hodgetts and Hodgetts (2020).

archaeologists are increasingly able to explore patterns of mobility, health, and demography on a population or supra-regional scale, as well as to unpick ever more complicated patterns of relatedness and connection at the local level.

Graves are one of the oldest sites of archaeological investigation. In part, this was because many ancient burials are visible on the surface – as mounds, megaliths, or other sorts of monument – and so attracted the attention of antiquaries and early archaeologists. However, and more significantly for the development of the field, grave assemblages are contexts in which the remains of one individual or more are incontrovertibly associated with one or more specific material objects. As such, they formed key elements of early relative chronologies and seriation models that attempted to sequence the introduction of new styles, artefacts, and materials and order them chronologically (as discussed in Section 2). The human remains also drew attention, with analysis focussing on interpretations of their lived identities based on the type and quantity of grave goods, the location or prominence of their burial, and the size and morphology of their physical features. Many of the early studies of the remains of past people were carried out within a (sometimes implicitly, sometimes explicitly) racist and colonialist framework, and we still grapple with that ugly legacy today (see the box 'Archaeology and Race').

ARCHAEOLOGY AND RACE

Early archaeologists and biological anthropologists (then frequently known as physical anthropologists) commonly believed in the fallacy that there were meaningful racial differences within the human population. Many believed that morphological differences in the human skeleton were evidence of these supposed racial differences, and we see attempts to delineate and describe the races of past people based on *craniometry* (the measurements of skulls) and other skeletal *morphometrics*.[107] Many of these practitioners amassed large reference collections of human remains, often taken clandestinely and put on display for prurient perusal by scientists and the public.

Among these was Samuel Morton, a physician interested in craniometric racial distinctions who built a collection of nearly 1,000 human crania in the early nineteenth century. His collection included First Nations people from the Americas, including people killed by

---

[107] Stout (2013).

the US Army during the so-called frontier wars, as well as crania from enslaved people, from immigrants, and from the impoverished.[108] Morton was a white supremacist who believed that different 'races' in fact represented different species, with non-white peoples being less human. He was not unique in his time, as scientific racism and eugenics were widely studied and quite respectable fields across the emerging social sciences in Europe and the Americas.[109] His legacy (and that of many contemporaries) forms part of the reason most bioarchaeologists reject the older moniker 'physical anthropology'; and the University of Pennsylvania, which holds his collection, continues to work (not always well) with descendant communities to repatriate and respectfully rebury the crania he appropriated.[110]

Archaeology has also been bound up with racist narratives and racecraft, both in its treatment of the ancestral remains of living people and in some of its historical practices and interpretations. Eighteenth-, nineteenth-, and early twentieth-century archaeologists were largely European or European descendant elites whose work enforced nation-alist ideals and who engaged directly in colonial extractivism. Museums are full of stolen material, and the processes of repatriation and restitution are still in their infancy. In the Americas, much early excavation was carried out by enslaved men and women, forced to dig burial mounds and other sites by plantation owners, including Thomas Jefferson.[111] In Europe, culture-historical attempts to trace specific peoples in the past were so powerfully racialised that they served as the foundations of the later Nazi pseudohistories.[112] The social evolu-tionary paradigm that dominated mainstream European and American culture in the nineteenth and twentieth centuries explicitly equated specific technological developments with social worth and level of humanity (Table 3)[113]. Where archaeological evidence was deemed too sophisticated or advanced to be the product of colonised peoples, elaborate explanations – often linked to biblical tales – were con-cocted. So, we have various 'lost tribes of Israel' deemed responsible for the construction of Great Zimbabwe, the Mississippian mounded settlements, and the great cities of the Maya world.

---

[108] Geller (2020). [109] Menand (2001). [110] Whelan and Greenberg (2022).
[111] Veit (1997). [112] Arnold (2006). [113] Morgan [1877] 1985; Tylor 1865

Table 3 Nineteenth-century evolutionary models of social and technological development set against the standard European archaeological periodisation which was developed contemporaneously.

| Tylor | Morgan | | |
Evolutionary stages	Evolutionary stages	Level of technological development	Archaeological ages
Savagery	Lower Savagery	Fruits and nuts, speech	Palaeolithic
	Middle Savagery	Fishing and gathering, use of fire	
	Upper Savagery	Hunting and gathering, bow and arrow, spear	
Barbarism	Lower Barbarism	Horticulture, pottery	Neolithic
	Middle Barbarism	Animal domestication (Eurasia), maize cultivation (Americas), irrigation, bronze smithing	
	Upper Barbarism	Cereal cultivation, iron smelting, wheeled vehicles, potter's wheel, loom weaving, poetry	Bronze Age
Civilisation	Ancient Civilisation	Iron-pointed ploughs, animal traction, coinage, hieroglyphic and phonetic alphabet, writing, cities	Iron Age/medieval era
	Modern Civilisation	Telegraph, power loom, steam engines, printing, gunpowder, photography, science democracy	Post-medieval era

These stories linger: the 'Mound Builders', as distinct from North American First Nations people, were debated well into the twentieth century, and this disinclination to give BIPOC people credit for the archaeological record also lies at the root of the Ancient Aliens myth. Several scientists and science writers have recently decried what they see as the re-emergence of scientific racism, especially around the communication and dissemination of genetic research.[114] Palaeogenomic studies are not immune, and archaeologists in particular are working hard to push geneticists studying the ancient past to take care not to feed into this perniciously persistent bigotry.[115]

[114] Rutherford (2022); Saini (2019).	[115] Frieman and Hofman (2019); Hakenbeck (2019).

The study of human remains is ethically complex. Until the last few decades, it was normal practice for archaeologists to excavate and study human remains with little or no consultation with local communities or descendant populations. The push to *repatriate* these remains, that is, to return them to their communities, is a major element of late twentieth- and twenty-first-century Indigenous sovereignty movements around the world.[116] Since the 1980s, there has been a major shift in our understanding of ethical practice in archaeology. Today, codes of ethics, such as the World Archaeology Congress' Vermillion Accord on human remains, instruct us to be respectful of both the living and the dead, to prioritise the perspectives of local and descendant communities in the treatment of human remains, and to work collaboratively to develop research projects that may or may not allow for the analysis of any human remains uncovered, although these are still only beginning to be fully adopted into the field.[117] Similar conversations are also ongoing about the ethics of displaying human remains in museums and other public fora.[118] Indeed, some philosophers and archaeologists now argue that we must take extra care working with human remains, not just because of an ethical imperative of respect and dignity for the living but also out of respect for those deceased people as formerly living beings in their own right.[119] This is particularly important as many cultures do not see the dead as absent from the world of the living but understand them as continuing to play active roles in living society for some time after their bodily death.[120]

Nevertheless, the analysis of human remains, termed variably *bioarchaeology* or *osteoarchaeology*, continues to be a major strand of archaeological research. Specialists study human remains to learn about individual deceased people as well as to develop a wider understanding of population-level phenomena, most prominently health, demography, and human evolution (see the box 'Finding Our Cousins'). Macroscopic analysis of bones and teeth can identify lesions that result from specific diseases, healed breakage, and malnourishment; dental illnesses, such as caries or cavities, often linked to restricted, high-carbohydrate diets; and changes in bone density related to musculature and habitual activities. Microscopic analysis includes biomolecular studies of stable isotopes of carbon, nitrogen, oxygen and strontium in teeth and bones that offer us information about an individual's diet and mobility in life as well as studies of bone histology to understand bone formation and remodelling and gain insight into health and illness visible at a cellular level.

---

[116] Fforde (2004).   [117] Squires et al. (2019).   [118] Biers (2019).
[119] Scarre (2003); Tarlow (2006).   [120] Semple and Brookes (2020).

The study of human evolution is one of the most rapidly evolving areas in biological anthropology. The pace of discoveries is high, thanks in part to the emergence of a suite of new techniques to identify, date, and analyse increasingly small fossils and osseous remains. The first cousin of ours to be identified was *Homo neanderthalensis*.[121] In 1856, disarticulated remains of three or more individuals were recovered from a cave in Neander Valley (North Rhine-Westphalia, Germany) by Johann Carl Fuhlrott, a local schoolteacher, who, with assistance from the anatomist Hermann Schaaffhausen, identified them as an archaic human. Other Neanderthal bones had been recovered in earlier campaigns at other sites, but they had not been identified as a separate species. Painstaking excavation over the course of the twentieth century, primarily in various locales in Africa, followed by careful anatomical and osteological analysis of fossils revealed further hominins and more distantly related kin.[122] These include the Australopithecines (such as the famous fossil 'Lucy' an *Australopithecus afarensis* recovered in Ethiopia and dated to about 3 million years old), Ardipithecus, and Paranthropus. In recent years, computational methods and 3D modelling have joined the methods applied by palaeoanthropologists to study fossils. Studies of ancient DNA and proteins (*proteomics*) have further increased (and complicated) our understanding of these cousin species and their relation to ourselves.

Consequently, our understanding of our hominin and earlier ancestry is regularly in a state of flux (Figure 15).[123] The current view is that we, *Homo sapiens*, emerged in Africa around 300,000 years ago, probably as a descendant of *H. erectus*. *H. erectus* was a highly mobile species, and their remains (and stone tools) are found across Eurasia. Many of our hominin cousins have been identified in Africa and Eurasia, most overlapping for thousands or millions of years with each other, though some are only known from singular sites or fossils. In Eurasia, *H. heidelbergensis* and *H. neanderthalensis* developed in the west and Denisovans in the east. In the last two decades, archaeologists have identified two further hominin species – *H. floresiensis* and *H. luzonensis* – in Indonesia and the Philippines, respectively, as well as other African hominins, such as *H. naledi*. Genetic research has demonstrated that these species not only overlapped in time and space but were manifestly capable of productive interbreeding, since all living human populations retain some genetic

---

[121] Madison (2016). [122] Goodrum (2009); Leakey (1979).
[123] For a recent review, see Bergström et al. (2021).

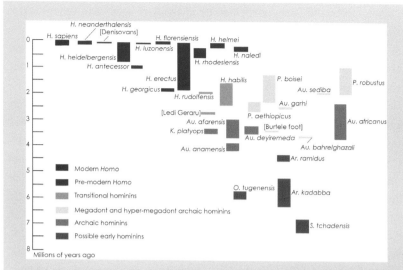

Figure 15 A taxonomy of hominin species (redrawn with alterations after Wood and Boyle 2016, fig. 1).

material from *H. neanderthalensis* and Denisovans as well as at least one 'ghost population', representing interbreeding that took place before our species left the African continent.[124]

Across Eurasia, physiological indicators of stress and new pathogens appear during the Neolithic among the earliest farming communities. Farming could be a precarious way of life, and the increasing density of settlements – as well as cohabitation of people and animals – put pressure on food systems to supply a growing population and led to the emergence of novel zoonoses. For example, Larsen and colleagues studied the human remains of nearly 1,000 individuals from Çatalhöyük, a well-known Neolithic settlement on the Konya Plain in Türkiye that was continuously occupied from the eighth to sixth millennium BCE – that is, the very early to middle Anatolian Neolithic.[125] Biomechanical analysis of the human remains indicates that the lifestyle was increasingly onerous over time – likely reflecting increasing amounts of labour and mobility linked to changes in animal herding practices and increased travel to access food and other resources. Moreover, dental analysis indicates the nearly universal presence of dental pathology resulting from regular periods of privation in childhood throughout the entire 1,200-year occupation of the site. Caries are present in 10 per cent of individuals, a result of the high-carbohydrate diet consumed by

---

[124] Durvasula and Sankararaman (2020).   [125] Larsen et al. (2015); Larsen et al. (2019).

the site's inhabitants, data confirmed by analysis of seeds and other macro-botanical remains that indicate very high quantities of wheat and other grain varieties at the site. Microscopic analysis of soil samples also yielded abundant evidence for parasites and parasite eggs which probably infected both the site's human and sheep occupants.

Broader studies into Neolithic *palaeodemography* and *palaeopathology* suggest that these were not isolated patterns. Among western European populations, cribra orbitalia and porotic hyperostosis lesions became widespread, although they are largely absent in earlier groups.[126] These are thought to reflect episodes of malnutrition, disease, and anaemia, although their aetiology may be complex.[127] Naugler previously linked anaemia to Neolithic high-grain diets,[128] though infection may be another cause. Ash and colleagues note that very early Neolithic individuals in western Europe seemed to have experienced more episodes of stress than eastern populations, though *sub-adults* (children and adolescents) in eastern areas may have been weaned earlier, leading to more nutritional stress in childhood in these populations.[129] Goude and colleagues looked at the isotopic evidence of diet in the teeth of prehistoric people from Liguria, Italy, and deduced that weaning times shrank distinctly in the Neolithic and again in the metal ages, with concomitant changes in diet and a reduction in health of infants and sub-adults, especially when they were weaned with low-protein vegetable diets.[130] Wittwer-Backhofen and Tomo observed a clear increase in dental caries among central European individuals from the Mesolithic to the Neolithic, as well as a period of high stress in the very early Neolithic.[131] These signs of childhood malnutrition suggest that mothers were under considerable nutritional stress during pregnancy. They suggest some of this stress might relate to sex-specific diets in which women ate more grain and less protein than men. The opposite pattern is identified in Greece by Papathanasiou, who sees a relatively healthy early Neolithic population become increasingly sick and malnourished over the course of the Neolithic.[132] She attributes this to a strong shift to terrestrial diets (and away from abundant coastal resources) as well as increasingly dense settlement practices. She considers this pattern in line with evidence from Neolithic populations around the eastern Mediterranean. Globally, much variation has been observed in the health impacts of the transition to agriculture.[133]

These analyses provide a rich insight into the lives and experiences of past people; but, like other classes of archaeological data, we must take care when

---

[126] McCullough et al. (2015: 47).   [127] Walker et al. (2009).   [128] Naugler (2008).
[129] Ash et al. (2016).   [130] Goude et al. (2020).   [131] Wittwer-Backofen and Tomo (2008).
[132] Papathanasiou (2011).   [133] Stock et al. (2023).

generalising from a handful of individuals to a whole society consisting of many people who were not buried in archaeologically visible ways or simply not recovered by archaeologists. In particular, bioarchaeologists argue that when we are constructing palaeodemographic and palaeopathological models we must always be aware of the *osteological paradox*. Following the foundational work by Wood and colleagues,[134] in attempting to abstract from an assemblage of human remains collected archaeologically to the living population of which they once formed part, we must take into account three factors:

- *Demographic non-stationarity*: The living population structure is dynamic and may fluctuate due to migration or changing fertility, but a funerary assemblage represents a static population over the time it was formed.
- *Selective mortality*: Skeletal samples are biased in representing the dead not the living since our study population consists of those most susceptible to death, that is, the most vulnerable individuals, at any given age; so, the prevalence of injury or illness among them is by definition not representative of the living population because all members of the study population are already in the worst possible state of health: dead.
- *Hidden heterogeneity in risks*: Prevalence rates estimated from this biased population do not capture the heterogeneity in susceptibility to disease (*morbidity*) and death (*mortality*) between individuals in a living population. Moreover, the presence or absence of bone lesions resulting from disease cannot be equated to the presence or absence of disease (as a person may die of an illness before bone lesions form) or the proportion of living individuals afflicted by this disease and their risk of dying from it.

The identification of the osteological paradox galvanised biological anthropology research, leading to new developments in cross-disciplinary analysis, mathematical modelling, human development, and biological processes as well as the integration of new data sources.[135] Among these, is ancient DNA (*aDNA*). *Palaeogenomic* research, a part of the historical sciences since the 1980s, has recently become increasingly important as our analytical methods improve (and the cost of analysis drops concomitantly) (see the box 'Gene Flow and Human Mobility'). In studies of palaeodemography and health, aDNA can help us identify pathogens in individuals who had not formed bone lesions or were not otherwise identifiable. Researchers have used this technique to identify past individuals who carried (and perhaps died from) tuberculosis, Hansen's disease (leprosy), and plague, among other diseases.[136]

---

[134] Wood et al. (1992).   [135] Grauer (2018).   [136] Cessford et al. (2021); Donoghue (2019).

GENE FLOW AND HUMAN MOBILITY

Genetic data provide an increasingly important source of information about past people and environments. Although geneticists have been studying past populations for decades, technological developments in the mid-2000s have led to an explosion of new research as they have opened up smaller and less well-preserved samples for sequencing. There are several different strands to this research, among them tracing the evolution of modern humans;[137] developing an understanding of the historical gene flow processes that led to modern population structure (i.e., the geographic patterning of genetic differences in the contemporary human population);[138] in-depth studies of palaeoenvironments and non-human species;[139] and, increasingly, how biological data can give us insights into historic and prehistoric social processes.[140]

Palaeogenomic research offers us a unique insight into histories of mobility since we can trace the movements of individuals and groups in their descendants' genetic code. This research typically focusses on either lineages of Y-chromosome or mitochondrial DNA (*mtDNA*), which allow us to determine paternal and material lineage, respectively; or it concerns whole genome analysis. Whole genome studies usually entail the identification of *single nucleotide polymorphisms* (*SNPs*), very short segments of DNA that are highly variable across the human genome, whose prevalence can be mapped geographically. Researchers in the Pacific, for example, have looked at the distribution of SNPs in populations from around Oceania to better understand the origin and distribution of the multiple waves of people who spread out into the various Pacific archipelagos from New Guinea and Island Southeast Asia.[141] Liu and colleagues go further by comparing the whole genome data to patterns of X-chromosome and mtDNA within Micronesian populations to argue that much of the Papuan ancestry in their sample derived from male migrants moving into Micronesia, while female migrants seem to have been few in number. Some gene flow patterns in the Pacific have been correlated with linguistic and archaeological data, providing numerical dates for some migration phases and allowing for interpretation of the impacts of population mobility on Oceanian societies.[142] However, one must remember these are correlated not causative: linguistic history (like all social practice) is not

---

[137] For example, Teixeira et al. (2021). [138] For example, Novembre et al. (2008).
[139] Crump (2021); Librado et al. (2021). [140] For example, Reich (2019).
[141] Choin et al. (2021); Liu et al. (2022). [142] Lipson et al. (2018).

determined by genetic ancestry, and having Papuan ancestry does not mean one speaks a Papuan language.[143]

The rapid emergence of ancient DNA research has become a topic of intense debate within archaeology. While, on the one hand, palaeogenomic research has led to exciting new insights about interpersonal relations or patterns of contact and mobility over time, on the other geneticists have struggled to adapt to the idiosyncrasies of archaeological data and the complex patterns of social relation embedded within them.[144] Palaeogenomics has accurately been accused of inadvertently reproducing outdated, sexist, and racist models because of biologists' lack of training in the human sciences and failure to collaborate with descendant communities;[145] but increasing and increasingly meaningful collaboration across disciplines is improving this situation.[146]

Integrating these biological data into archaeological narratives is not always easy. Indeed, as we have seen, the interpretation of any archaeological remains is rarely straightforward because the material itself is complicated, intrinsically fragmented, and rarely accompanied by writing or images that document its use and meaning. Funerary contexts, the source of most of the human remains we study, are no different due both to problems of preservation and recovery and to social factors. Moreover, in the past, even where bones were well-preserved, archaeologists may not have retained the material they excavated or may only have retained selected bones, such as the crania, or selected individuals from a funerary assemblage, meaning that legacy collections in museums are often incomplete.

For much of the history of funerary archaeology, grave goods – objects found in the grave with bodies – and funerary architecture were the primary media studied to give us insights into the lived experiences or identity of the deceased person, with the orientation or layout of human remains and their spatial relation to each other forming another key data source.[147] Cooper and colleagues trace the role of grave goods in social interpretation to mid-nineteenth-century attempts to delineate separate groups of people and their movements by shared sets of material culture or funerary rite, an early form of the culture-historical approach.[148] In the later twentieth century, as radiocarbon dating replaced finely

---

[143] Posth et al. (2018).   [144] Booth (2019); Brück (2021); Crellin and Harris (2020).
[145] Fox and Hawkes (2019); Frieman and Hofmann (2019); Frieman et al. (2019); Tsosie et al. (2020).
[146] Alpaslan-Roodenberg et al. (2021); Booth et al. (2021); Spriggs and Reich (2019).
[147] Parker Pearson (1999: 1–20); Sofaer (2006: 12).
[148] Cooper et al. (2022: 11–44); Trigger (2006: 211–313).

detailed sequences of artefacts and culture groups, more attention was paid to the variety, quality, and potential significance of the materials, rites, and funerary architecture uncovered by archaeologists at different times and places. Instead of delineating peoples, archaeologists began to delineate statuses or ranks held by individuals, basing their interpretation heavily in ethnographic analogies. The quantity of grave goods, size of the funerary monument, variety of materials, complexity of the mortuary rite, association with other human remains, and so on were all used to order individuals from lowest to highest status and, moreover, to order their societies from least to most complex in the evolutionary paradigms that were dominant at the time.[149]

Advances in skeletal analysis and biomolecular research as well as shifts in interpretative practice away from broad evolutionary modelling and towards smaller-scale, social theory–influenced approaches have seen the field of mortuary archaeology change radically since the 1980s. However, many archaeologists continue to develop interpretations of social structure, cosmology, and stratification based on patterns of funerary deposition and the layout of individuals, grave groups, and larger funerary landscapes. The early medieval specialist Duncan Sayer, for example, outlines a complex model of early medieval kinship, personal and household identity, and social transformation through the detailed analysis of more than 100 cemeteries dating from the fifth to eighth century CE.[150] He primarily focusses on the horizontal layouts of these sites but develops a nuanced discussion of gender, household, community, and local history through a holistic analysis of furnished and unfurnished graves, careful study of grave goods, and close attention to sequences of deposition and the succession of localised funerary rites.

The last few decades have seen the emergence of the subfield of *archaeothanatology*, a school of research that treats the funerary site as the locus of multiple ongoing and dynamic taphonomic processes, biological, geological and social, that must be disentangled in order to understand the affordances, significance, and representativeness of the human remains.[151] For example, different soil conditions and geological environments affect the survival of osseous material; so, in some situations no, few, or only the most robust skeletal elements (e.g., tooth enamel) will survive any length of time in the ground. This obviously has impacts on where archaeologists are able to recover material for study and which analyses (if any) they are able to carry out. Social practices also impact on recovery and preservation. The choice to cremate, for example, influences the amount of bone that may be preserved and the analyses which

---

[149] Chapman (2013).   [150] Sayer (2020).
[151] Duday et al. (2009); Knüsel and Schotsmans (2021).

can be conducted on it. Funerary rites that include excarnation (exposure of the remains) or dismemberment might result in fragmentation commencing prior to inhumation. The location of deposition – in plain air, in caves, in waterways, in the ground – obviously shapes what material archaeologists can access, as does the choice of who to bury. At most times in the past, only a small proportion of the population were accorded funerary rites of the sort that would ensure their remains survived, and only a small portion of these have been recovered archaeologically.

Furthermore, despite the long history of studying grave goods and funerary architecture, these are also imperfect mirrors. Burials are emotionally powerful social events created and enacted by the living within the constraints of their established social practice and which may communicate information about a given decedent; but they are also performances designed for those still alive.[152] So, the grave goods that accompany a person in death may reflect their status and lived identity, but they may just as well also represent gifts from still living kin, ritual objects necessary for the success of the rites themselves but with no connection to the decedent, or displays of status by new or emerging leaders, such as the public destruction or deposition of large amounts of wealth.

Taking our lead from bioarchaeology, we might perhaps consider these constraints to interpretation a sort of *archaeothanatological paradox* (Figure 16) that requires us to take into account:

- *Survival non-uniformity*: Various taphonomic processes (natural and social) differentially affect the survival of human remains, leaving us with a patchy and uneven data set and one that can be somewhere on a continuum between highly skewed by these processes to functionally random.
- *Selective deposition*: Only a segment of any population – and sometimes quite a small one – was interred in archaeologically visible ways; so, by using funerary data as a key source for modelling past identities and social practices, we are drawing normative conclusions from social outliers.
- *Social heterogeneity in rites*: The funerary record is all that remains of a variety of tangible and intangible social practices that are performed or enacted by living communities around the death or deposition of a person or persons. These may engage with aspects of the decedent's identity in life, or they may draw on wider understandings of their role or position, or they may respond to other social pressures entirely and have little to nothing to do with the deceased person's own identity or relations. Funerary sites are carefully assembled in these rites, highly variable, and temporally flattened

---

[152] Parker Pearson (1999: 3).

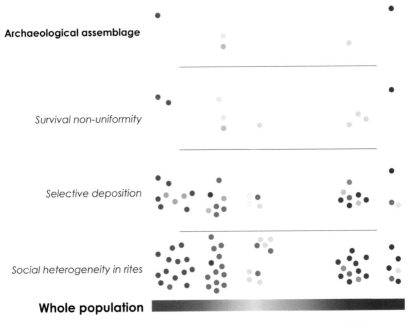

Figure 16 The archaeothanatological paradox that shapes our ability to
reconstruct living populations from funerary populations.

since considerable time may elapse between a person's bodily and social
deaths.

Although these seem like major hurdles, an archaeothanatological approach
offers us a methodological framework to navigate this extremely complex and
ambiguous body of data. It advocates a mix of detailed field documentation of
the *in situ* skeletal elements, their orientation, and their spatial relation to their
wider context in order to delineate the various natural and social processes that
impacted the mortuary site and the human remains themselves.[153] These field
observations can be combined with experimental research (e.g., on decay
processes in different environments or after specific funerary treatments),
laboratory analysis of excavated skeletal material, palaeoecological and geological data, and so on.

For example, Solari and colleagues set out to distinguish among funerary
practices, accidental post-depositional interference, and intentional post-
funerary manipulation and to disambiguate anthropogenic grave disturbance
from natural taphonomic processes at four Mid-to-Late Holocene cemetery
sites in north-east Brazil.[154] All four sites had what had been termed

---

[153] Duday et al. (2009).   [154] Solari et al. (2022).

'anomalous' burials, that is, burials that did not conform to the presumed normative practice of single inhumation burials. These included burials with evidence of burning, burials of more than one individual, and burials that appeared to have been disarticulated. Solari and colleagues combined careful field analysis of the archaeological contexts and natural processes (e.g., disturbance by roots or insects, soil formation processes) with robust laboratory work, including macroscopic and microscopic analysis of the skeletal material. This enabled them to distinguish between natural disturbance, such as termite burrows or the decay caused by acidic soils, and what they term 'post-funerary cycles' of action, such as the intentional disarticulation of bodies after their initial funerary deposition and the secondary reburial of partial human remains. They conclude that declaring some burials normative and others anomalous in Holocene Brazil, in fact, conceals a systematically widespread and quite long-lasting set of complex social practices that linked post-burial interventions to ongoing funerary rites. This approach both makes sense of complicated mortuary contexts and offers us new avenues of social interpretation focussed on people's apparently regular and repeated interaction with the bodies of the long-deceased.

5 Telling Stories That Change the World

While the public often imagines archaeology as a discipline devoted to times long past, many archaeologists today carry out research with the problems of the contemporary world in mind. A major part of the so-called post-processual critique of the 1980s – a movement critical of positivist and scientific modes of interpretation – was the suggestion that how we interpret the past is political. Michael Shanks and Chris Tilley made the influential case that archaeological interpretation is shaped by the political and social (and economic, environmental, etc.) contexts in which it is carried out: that is, how we read the past is entirely dependent on the world in which we live. They argued that the power imbalances within the dominant society experienced by most archaeologists (e. g., middle-class, white, and Euro-American) are read into the past by unreflective archaeologists who use common wisdom to recreate their own status quo with the detritus of past worlds.[155] More scientific archaeologists (who were the focus of Shanks and Tilley's critiques) objected to their vision of the past,[156] but the assertion that the past holds power, that our interpretations have resonance in the present, and that this can be operationalised to achieve tangible changes in the contemporary world has been widely accepted.[157]

---

[155] Shanks and Tilley (1987).   [156] For example, Watson (1990).   [157] Stahl (2022).

Certainly, we know that archaeology can do harm. Infamously, archaeology was heavily promoted and well-funded by the mid-twentieth-century Nazi regime, because they sought justification for their racism and invasions in archaeological narratives of identity and migration.[158] This was not unique to the Nazis, as archaeology has been bound up with nationalism and the colonial nation-state more or less since its emergence as a distinct discipline.[159] As discussed in previous sections, archaeological research carried out by Europeans in the lands they colonised too often followed the same extractivist ideology that informed their imperial expansion and reinforced pre-existing ideas about social complexity, power, and cultural valour.

In recent years, we have seen a concerted effort by right-wing reactionaries and political parties to use historical and archaeological pasts to bolster their claims of racial and ethnic purity and legitimise their claims to power.[160] In 2017, white supremacists marching in Charlottesville, Virginia, brandished Viking runes and other early medieval symbols much the way mid-twentieth-century Nazis looked to the Iron and Bronze Ages of Scandinavia for their origins. Beyond symbolising a fictive, white ancestry, this display of ancient symbols was also a claim to territory: many white supremacists argue that Vikings who settled in North America are the true Indigenous people of the continent; and, thus, these supposedly Viking-descended white supremacists have first claim to the land and its domination.[161] L'Anse aux Meadows in Newfoundland, Canada, is the only confirmed Viking site in North America, and it was not a permanent settlement but seems to have been occupied seasonally for a few summers in the tenth and eleventh centuries CE.[162]

Less maliciously, the long history of archaeological research in Europe has clearly contributed to European people's own ideas of their ethnicity, identity, and cultural distinction.[163] Unfortunately this opens the door to emotive manipulation of the past by political actors. Recent years have seen conservative and centrist political parties use the deep past to claim a lineage for the status quo and justify land tenure and domination by a small subset of the population.[164] In England during the 2019 election, the notorious conservative politician Jacob Rees-Mogg filmed a political advertisement in front of a 5,000-year-old stone circle in his constituency, visually and verbally tying his politics to the deep past of the area (Figure 17). The archaeologist Kenny Brophy has documented numerous examples of British politicians invoking the archaeological record of the United Kingdom, especially iconic sites like Stonehenge,

---

[158] Arnold (1990); Härke (2014).   [159] Díaz-Andreu García (2007); Trigger (1984).
[160] Hofmann et al. (2021).   [161] Livingstone (2017).   [162] Kuitems et al. (2021).
[163] Graves-Brown et al. (1996).   [164] Niklasson and Hølleland (2018).

We must get Brexit done, it is time for the Common Market to leave Stanton Drew. Only the Conservatives can do that. #VoteConservative

Dec 2, 2019

Figure 17 Screenshot of a tweet from 2 December 2019 by the English Conservative politician Jacob Rees-Mogg with a party political video shot at Stanton Drew stone circle. The tweet has since been deleted.

while justifying their support for the UK's departure from the European Union, a manipulation of the past he terms 'Brexit Prehistory'.[165]

The way the past acts in the present need not be to support nationalist or racist narratives. Feminist and queer activists argue that the past offers us examples and space to critique contemporary inequalities based on gender and sexuality.[166] The last two decades have furnished multiple examples of archaeological research that embeds a queer perspective, not just identifying individual queer people or social categories in the past but also breaking down the heteronormative categories and logics embedded in archaeological interpretation.[167] Eschewing heteronormativity allows us to identify non-binary sexualities and individuals in the past,[168] so two individuals buried together, each with a sword, might well have been lovers as well as brothers in arms.[169]

Moreover, recognising that queer and non-binary people have been present at all times and in all societies gives us insight into those social and historical practices that sought to erase them, including European colonialism,[170] while also offering archaeologists a privileged platform to

---

[165] Brophy (2018, 2019). [166] Conkey and Gero (1997); Voss (2000).
[167] Dowson (2000); Voss (2008). [168] Frieman et al. (2019). [169] Walsh et al. (2022).
[170] TallBear (2018); Voss and Casella (2012).

push back against contemporary inequalities, such as the transphobic lie that gender diversity is recent. Archaeology tells us that trans and gender-diverse people have always existed and that gender expression and sexual practices are mutable, shifting, and historically and culturally contingent.[171] Similarly, despite archaeology's historical entanglement with colonialism and white supremacy, a rising generation of Indigenous and First Nations archaeologists are redefining the discipline, using archaeological practice to reconnect with their own heritage and creating a framework in which archaeological data are put to work to support Indigenous dignity and sovereignty (see the box 'Indigenous and First Nations archaeologies').

INDIGENOUS AND FIRST NATIONS ARCHAEOLOGIES

The increasing number and growing prominence of Indigenous or First Nations archaeologists and their approach to the study of the past are challenging some of the basic tenets of the field. Trust between First Nations communities and archaeologists has historically been fragile, with the Aboriginal Tasmanian activist Ros Langford famously deriding archaeology as the practice of making one's reputation on the graves of Indigenous people.[172] The Standing Rock Sioux activist and historian Vine Deloria, Jr. echoed these remarks about a decade later, though he struck a slightly more optimistic tone by identifying areas, such as the recording of selected sacred sites, where archaeologists could work with and for First Nations communities.[173]

In the subsequent decades, most archaeologists have embraced this approach, making direct collaboration with Indigenous communities a core feature of ethical practice.[174] In Australia and North America, best practice requires consultation with communities at every stage of a project, collaboration to develop appropriate research questions, and respect for their decisions regardless of specific research interests.[175] Commercial development, of course, complicates these relationships.[176] Moreover, field schools and other training opportunities are increasingly inviting Indigenous leadership and participation, blurring the line between community members and archaeologist and making space for interpretation and investigation that do not centre western scientific assumptions but flow on from Indigenous knowledge.[177]

---

[171] Black Trowel Collective (2021); Weismantel (2013).   [172] Langford (1983).
[173] Deloria (1992).   [174] Colwell-Chanthaphonh et al. (2010); Johnston (2004).
[175] Atalay (2012); Smith et al. (2019).   [176] Costello (2021).
[177] Gonzalez and Edwards (2020); May, Marshall et al. (2017).

Although archaeology in Europe and the anglosphere is still over-whelmingly white, increasing numbers of Indigenous and First Nations students are studying archaeology and making the field their own. The Métis archaeologist Kisha Supernant has described how doing archaeology and studying the historic Métis landscape have brought her into better relation with her own heritage and identity.[178] She studies Métis pasts to better understand the daily life, experiences, and humanity of Métis people, 'to engage in relentless remembering and reminding through the physical remains of the past' to counter the ongoing white settlement of her people's land and history.[179] In Australia, Indigenous archaeologists have vocally opposed government and heritage structures that allow for the destruction of important cultural sites by, for example, multinational mining companies and called for greater recognition of Indigenous sovereignty – both over the land and over their own histories and heritage.[180] Indigenous data sovereignty includes control over the collection and use of First Nations people's genomic material, and Indigenous scientists and biological anthropologists have offered ethical guidelines and best-practice case studies for archaeologists seeking to study Indigenous DNA.[181] As the proportion of Indigenous archaeologists increases, these changes to the underlying assumptions, day-to-day practices, and ethics of archaeology are shifting the discipline away from one that benefits by taking knowledge from First Nations communities to one that flourishes only insofar as it benefits these communities directly.[182]

Historical and contemporary archaeologies – subdisciplines that emerged in the later twentieth century – are focussed on the recent past, with a particular interest in the archaeology of colonialism, marginalised peoples, and the working classes. In these fields, we see the tools of archaeology employed alongside ethnography, oral history, and written texts to document and interpret a world not captured by mainstream media or recounted in dominant historical narratives. Alfredo González-Ruibal refers to the period since the First World War as that of 'supermodernity' and argues that archaeologists, as experts in ruins and death, have a special role to play in understanding and interpreting a period of unprecedented global violence, trauma, and destructiveness.[183] Historical and

---

[178] Supernant (2020a: 94).   [179] Supernant (2020a: 106).
[180] Koolmatrie (2020); Wilson in Smith et al. (2019).
[181] Claw et al. (2018); Tsosie et al. (2020).   [182] Laluk et al. (2022).
[183] González-Ruibal (2008, 2019).

contemporary archaeologists, for example, are leading researchers studying recent warfare, genocide, and their victims and perpetrators.[184] This research is conducted not to titillate but to render tangible recent atrocities so that victims may be repatriated, perpetrators condemned, and the social and political contexts that allowed these atrocities to occur revealed in hopes they are not replicated elsewhere (see the box 'Unearthing Atrocities').

UNEARTHING ATROCITIES

The excavation of mass graves is not new to archaeology. Since the 1980s, archaeologists have been developing methods for the precise, scientific, and respectful excavation of the victims of recent violence.[185] These include victims of genocide, warfare, and natural disasters that took place anywhere in the last 200 years, though often the violence is quite recent. The 1990s, for example, saw archaeological excavations to unearth mass graves related to episodes of genocidal ethnic cleansing in central Africa and south-east Europe. These excavations served two roles: to identify individuals so their remains might be returned to their communities and to furnish evidence for historical narratives and legal tribunals.[186] Local communities are often aware of these sites prior to their excavation – some may remember the atrocities themselves – but excavation of the remains makes this difficult history tangible, rendering past crimes inescapably real and forcing us to reckon with their perpetrators.[187]

The archaeology of sites of mass death and atrocity is innately difficult, but it is also a powerful practice that disrupts dominant historical narratives and gives descendant communities greater agency, both in the retelling of their histories and in their ability to fight for a better future. Edward González-Tennant, for example, used GIS landscape models and excavation to explore the 1923 massacre of Black people and wholesale destruction of Black-owned businesses in Rosewood, Florida.[188] He created 3D models and other public-facing heritage materials in collaboration with the local community, including Rosewood descendants and massacre survivors. His archaeological methodology for studying race riots recognises both that these events are rarely fully documented in their own time and that they nonetheless continue to resonate through generations in large and small ways. A current project directed by Alicia Odewale in partnership with the local community is using archaeological methods to study the 1921 massacre in Tulsa, Oklahoma, in which hundreds of people were killed

---

[184] Bernbeck and Pollock (2007).   [185] Skinner (1987); Steele (2008).
[186] Haglund et al. (2001: 57).   [187] Bernbeck and Pollock (2007); Košir (2020: 268).
[188] González-Tennant (2018).

and Greenwood, a prosperous Black community, was destroyed.[189] Odewale describes this as a liberatory project enhanced by an archaeological approach, since archaeology affords 'multiple truths be able to coexist in the same space'.[190]

In 2021, white Canadians were shocked to learn of the discovery of hundreds of unmarked children's graves on the grounds of former residential schools that once housed thousands of First Nations children.[191] These institutions were established across Canada and largely run by religious organisations with the aim of Christianising and assimilating First Nations children who had been forcibly removed from their families.[192] This cultural genocide was accompanied by a singularly callous attitude towards their physical health and well-being, leading to scores of deaths from illness, neglect, and starvation. Archaeologists working with and for First Nations communities are using remote sensing, including ground-penetrating radar, to confirm the location of mass graves identified by residential school survivors and to quantify them. While First Nations communities have long known the location of these unmarked graves, this new archaeological evidence is forcing white North Americans and cultural elites to confront the scale of mass child death in these institutions for the first time. Even in an early stage, the impact of this collaborative research is already clear in new government initiatives and community responses.[193]

The archaeology of the recent past is also the archaeology of invasion, of child labour, of slavery, of forced migrants, and of poverty. Historical and contemporary archaeologists frequently use their insights into these undocumented histories to tell stories that counter our contemporary world view in order to make space for marginalised people. Sally K. May and colleagues' work on so-called Contact rock art in Australia, that is, rock art produced by Aboriginal Australians during the process of European colonialism (predominantly nineteenth- and twentieth-century), explores Indigenous responses to colonial incursions as articulated among and between other Indigenous people, rather than documented by white outsiders (see the box 'Co-creating Knowledge with Indigenous Communities' in Section 2).[194] Their work highlights the ways traditional practices, including art-making and ceremony, were used to interpret introduced materials, educate each other about them and about

---

[189] Alicia Odewale and Karla Slocum. '#Tulsasyllabus: The Rise, Destruction, and Rebuilding of Tulsa's Greenwood District', https://tulsasyllabus.web.unc.edu/.
[190] Quoted in Gannon (2020). [191] Austen (2021). [192] Supernant (2020b).
[193] Bryden (2021); US Department of the Interior (2021).
[194] May, Taçon et al. (2021); May et al. (2020); May, Wesley et al. (2017).

the invading colonisers, and create space for cultural practices to be retained even in the face of genocide.

In a more contemporary context, the archaeologist Gabriel Moshenska and the community activist Shaun Shelly conducted an archaeological analysis of discarded illicit drug paraphernalia in order to re-humanise and render visible injecting drug users who are frequently excluded not just from contemporary society but also from archaeological narratives of the recent past.[195] This project builds on foundational research by Rachael Kiddey, developed in collaboration with unhoused communities.[196] Kiddey and colleagues mapped the landscapes of unhoused people in Bristol and York in the United Kingdom, recording social relations and significant places, then collectively excavating and interpreting two of the latter. This research not only added to the wider understanding of how unhoused people navigate British urban spaces and make places and communities of their own but also had a meaningful impact on the unhoused collaborators, who reported a wealth of personal benefits from increased self-confidence to a strong sense of empowerment and inclusion.

This research is explicitly part of a new activist paradigm of archaeological practice that has emerged in the last two decades and advocates direct action by archaeologists and through the tools and methods of archaeology.[197] Atalay and colleagues define such activist archaeology as 'an archaeology that has dual loyalties to communities of archaeologists and to communities of non-archaeologists who value the past and welcome opportunities to harness archaeology to address contemporary social, economic, and political concerns'.[198] They call for archaeologists to work with respect and trust towards social and environmental justice, sustainability, equity, knowledge democratisation, and Indigenous sovereignty. Stottman identifies the origin of the activist impulse in the practice of public archaeology, that is, archaeology carried out with public education in mind.[199] Since the 1980s, and with greater impact and intensity since 2000, public archaeology has transformed into community archaeology – archaeology by and with communities. This approach to fieldwork is increasingly supported by local governments, heritage organisations, and funding bodies and has been demonstrated to benefit communities through increasing their local knowledge and enhancing community cohesion.[200]

These engaged archaeologies work with and for often marginalised groups to study their unique histories and work with them to develop heritage practices that empower them in the present.[201] Indeed, activist archaeologists work to

---

[195] Moshenska and Shelly (2020).   [196] Kiddey (2017).
[197] Atalay, Clauss, Welch et al. (2016); Sabloff (2008); Stottman (2010a).
[198] Atalay, Clauss, McGuire et al. (2016: 13).   [199] Stottman (2010b).
[200] Lewis et al. (2022).
[201] Atalay (2012); Kiddey (2020); Richardson and Almansa-Sánchez (2015).

address the problems of the contemporary world, to empower marginalised communities through archaeology and heritage practice, and to bring the deep-time perspectives offered by archaeology to bear on current debates (see the box 'Enacting Anarchism: The Black Trowel Collective').

ENACTING ANARCHISM: THE BLACK TROWEL COLLECTIVE

The Black Trowel Collective (BTC) was formed in 2016 by a group of archaeologists seeking to apply anarchist theory and methods to interpreting the past. These archaeologists were interested not just in anarchism as theory but also in building anarchist values, practices, and world views into their own daily life and how they do their archaeology (Figure 18).[202] Their manifesto articulates the principles of an anarchist archaeology: critiquing power, recognising and supporting resistance at the small and large scales, visioning futures, seeking non-authoritarian forms of organisation in the past but also in contemporary professional organising, recognising the heterogeneity of identities, exposing multiple scales from the bottom up, recognising agency in change and stability, valuing the heritage of state and non-state societies, encouraging a multitude of views and voices rather than adherence to strict paradigms, recognising relations with non-humans, and taking action to create a more equitable and more joyful world.[203]

In subsequent years, BTC members have published a considerable and increasing body of research exploring the interface of anarchism and archaeology and spurred an interest in these approaches by many non-members.[204] Some of this work has taken the form of re-evaluations of archaeological data. For example, James Flexner has examined non-state and heterarchical social and political organisation in the pre-Contact Pacific, arguing across a number of papers that the long-standing archaeological interest in political complexity and the emergence of state-level societies obscures more complicated and less top-down social structures through which people resisted both colonial hegemony and incipient inequality.[205] He and others also use an anarchist framework to explore how archaeologists create knowledge and to argue for the ways that an anarchist approach can help build a more sustainable and equitable future.[206]

Since 2020, the BTC has taken a more activist stance alongside its academic output. The year 2020 saw the launch of a mutual aid project,

---

[202] Borck and Sanger (2017). [203] Black Trowel Collective (2016).
[204] See the BTC-curated anarchist archaeology bibliography for an overview: https://blacktrowel collective.wordpress.com/anarchist-archaeology-bibliography/.
[205] Flexner (2014, 2020a). [206] Borck (2019); Flexner (2020b).

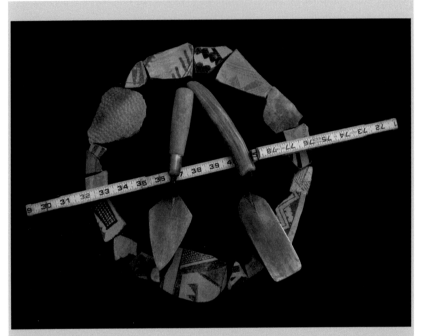

Figure 18 Vision of an anarchist archaeology (image by Lewis Borck, CC-BY-NC-SA 4.0).

which took the form of microgrants for archaeology students anywhere in the world. In the first two years, more than US$70,000 were disbursed, all from public donations.[207] The BTC has also put out position statements supporting Indigenous colleagues and arguing that archaeologists should work for trans liberation and celebrate a diversely gendered past, as well as producing a guide for running safe and respectful conference sessions and panels and a model consensus process.[208] All of this stems from the call to arms in the BTC manifesto to 'Do something big, or do something small.

---

[207] Black Trowel Collective (@Black Trowel), 'Happy Anniversary!', Twitter, 22 June 2021, 7:47 a.m., https://twitter.com/BlackTrowel/status/1407228625548713985).

[208] 'The Black Trowel Collective Stands in Solidarity with Our Indigenous Colleagues', Black Trowel Collective Microgrants (web post), 19 April 2021, https://blacktrowelcollective.word press.com/2021/04/19/the-black-trowel-collective-stands-in-solidarity-with-our-indigenous-colleagues/; 'Archaeologists for Trans Liberation', Black Trowel Collective Microgrants (web post), 6 July 2021, https://blacktrowelcollective.wordpress.com/2021/07/06/archaeologists-for-trans-liberation/; 'Running Safer Sessions', Black Trowel Collective Microgrants (web post), 14 January 2021, https://blacktrowelcollective.wordpress.com/2021/01/14/running-safer-sessions/; 'The Black Trowel Collective Consensus Process', Black Trowel Collective Microgrants (web post), 6 May 2021, https://blacktrowelcollective.wordpress.com/2021/05/06/black-trowel-collective-consensus-process/.

> Do something different. Write a classic. Do what feels right. Do it for archaeology's potential to help us build a better world. Make it grand. Make it humble. Make it brilliant.'

While feminist and queer archaeologists have been engaged in just these sorts of practices for nearly four decades, wider discourses about power, obligation, and inclusion are bringing activist practices into the archaeological mainstream, particularly among the increasing numbers of archaeologists from minority or minoritised backgrounds. In North America, in recent years, Black archaeologists have taken the lead in excavating and interpreting the archaeological traces of the African diaspora, both the mundane evidence of the daily life of Black people (free and unfree) and episodes of violent oppression.[209] In the 1990s, a survey of nearly 1,700 members of the Society of American Archaeology revealed only two who identified as Black, and anecdotal knowledge and personal networks only added two more.[210] This situation has improved, but Black people still make up less than 1 per cent of the thousands of archaeologists in North America, a situation common to other anglophone countries.[211]

The Society of Black Archaeologists (SBA) was founded in 2011 with a mission both to advance archaeological research into the African diaspora and to promote the field of archaeology among African descendant communities, including encouraging more Black people into the discipline.[212] The SBA has promoted this mission through scholarly as well as public venues. This has included the organisation of archaeological field schools that bring together Black archaeologists with Black community members, including schoolchildren,[213] and the co-organisation in 2020 and 2021 of a series of panel discussions on Black and Indigenous futures in archaeology.[214] Their work explicitly connects the study of the past and the contemporary experiences of people of African descent and sees archaeology as a key domain through which social justice can be achieved.

Archaeologists have also offered their knowledge, skills, and voices to the global climate activist movement. Archaeology, a research field that explores

---

[209] Franklin et al. (2020: 755–6). [210] Franklin (1997).
[211] Mate and Ulm (2021); White and Draycott (2020).
[212] 'Promoting Academic Excellence *and Social Responsibility*: About the Society of Black Archaeologists', Society of Black Archaeologists (SBA) website, www.societyofblackarchaeol ogists.com/about.
[213] Wade (2019).
[214] 'From the Margins to the Mainstream: Black and Indigenous Futures in Archaeology', 25 September 2020, *Sapiens* (online), www.sapiens.org/archaeology/black-and-indigenous-futures-in-archaeology/.

both social and natural environments – including the overlaps and entanglements between the two (see Section 1) – has a special role to play in characterising the Anthropocene and helping us chart a sustainable path to surviving our own excesses without succumbing to authoritarian and xenophobic impulses.[215] Palaeoclimate data allow us to characterise the nature of current climatic shifts and quantify their oscillations away from long-term patterns and offer proxy records for modelling future climates;[216] and a long-standing interest in social and technological change primes us to address social resilience, that is, how past people adapted (or did not) to rapid climatic changes.[217]

So, Fernández and colleagues explore a medieval village destroyed by flooding near the start of the Little Ice Age in the late thirteenth or early fourteenth century CE and identify the ways that local elites profited from this small-scale catastrophe.[218] More hopefully, Chelsea Fisher makes the case that archaeology can offer paths forward to achieve a sustainable future for agriculture.[219] Specifically, she suggests, first, that archaeological data on the myriad technologies and complex environmental impacts of past agricultural practices can guide us as we search for sustainable solutions to feed an ever-expanding human population and, second, that our interest in the domestic, small-scale, and practical elements of past lifeways offers special insights into how the technologies of agriculture are imbricated with interpersonal and social relations.

Beyond enhancing the scientific study of climate change and the Anthropocene, a number of archaeologists contend that we must use this special position between past and future to enhance the public's understanding of climate change and the ways we might face it in the future, especially as archaeological narratives are already widely consumed by non-specialists.[220] Finally, within the framework of sustainability studies, archaeologists have begun debating how to enact 'degrowth' strategies within our own field, to model how we and others might step away from capitalist imperatives to *do more, faster, and bigger* as well as to construct a more sustainable heritage industry for a difficult future.[221]

Conclusion

Every archaeologist has a unique origin story. Some join nearby excavations as children and slide naturally into the profession. Others fall in love with museums and spend hours of their childhood glued to glass cases, puzzling

---

[215] Pétursdóttir (2017); Rick and Sandweiss (2020).   [216] Riede (2014).
[217] Stahl (2022: 52–4); Van de Noort (2011).   [218] Fernández et al. (2019).
[219] Fisher (2020).   [220] Hudson et al. (2012: 322); Jackson et al. (2018).
[221] Flexner (2020b); Zorzin (2021).

out the objects within. Still others watch archaeology on TV and dream of their chance to be the person in front of the camera. Many discover archaeology at university, sometimes by accident, having followed a friend or a wonderful lecturer to a class they did not intend to take. A few come to archaeology late after years or even decades in another career. When I was thirteen years old, a teacher who knew my love for both history and fiction handed me a copy of James Michener's novel *The Source*.[222] This novel tells the story of the excavation of a Palestinian tell site, interweaving the excavation itself with the stories of the various past settlements being uncovered. Michener's protagonist, the site's lead archaeologist, starts the novel reflecting on his training and experience. He thinks about the other sites he had excavated, the skills he learned, and the classes he took in ceramics, ancient history, and a variety of other topics. For me, this brief scene served as a powerful lightbulb moment: archaeology, I realised, was something I could learn to do – it was a just a domain of knowledge and a series of techniques that anyone (very much including me) could learn.

Although we often focus on specific activities or subfields – excavation, ceramic analysis, ancient DNA – archaeology as a discipline is, at its core, a way of asking and answering questions about people and the worlds they built and inhabited (often in the past, but not always). It understands people as existing in complex relations with the material world and broader environment; and, through these relations, more ephemeral aspects of our society, practices, and relationships are materialised and become accessible for study. And yet, the data themselves are fragmentary and their reconstruction hypothetical. Two centuries of increasingly refined methods have made clear that no single site or artefact, no one date or burial, suffices. So, we work across domains, materialities, cultures, and temporalities. Moreover, every new site or artefact brings with it its own challenges, often unpredictable; so, we must also learn to be flexible in our approach, able to adapt our methods of excavation or analysis and adopt new techniques to answer the unexpected questions with which the archaeological record so frequently confronts us. We apply a host of scientific methods, borrow lines of enquiry from anthropology and sociology, and accept that our inferences will almost never be proved definitively right or wrong. This generates complex, multistranded narratives that braid together the results of laboratory work, comparisons to other sites or people, careful reflection on accumulated prior knowledge, and new hypotheses about what people may have been doing in a given place and time. And these stories we tell have power well beyond the simple satisfaction of curiosity about unknown worlds.

---

[222] Michener (1965).

Archaeology has always been about more than just piecing together the ancient past from bits of ceramic and broken rock. The scientific discipline was birthed alongside European colonialism and nationalism, and this legacy remains part of the field.[223] The drive to discover, to collect, to order, and to interpret that underpins many of archaeology's foundational methods cannot be extricated from the extractive practices of European settler colonialism which saw colonised countries as vast stores of wealth and resources, while colonised people were the savage remnants of a long-lost past. It is no surprise then that archaeological research has formed part of racist, colonialist, and explicitly fascist political movements. We are still establishing an ethical best practice for the field, a task with no obvious end point as archaeology continues to absorb new methods and specialisms that require careful consideration. However, recent years have seen archaeologists from around the world embrace the powerful connection archaeology offers between past and present to push for a better, more equitable future. Black and Indigenous archaeologists are creating space for their own knowledge, histories, and ways of relating to flourish. Anarchists and other activists argue that archaeology can provide hope and the possibility to reshape a world rapidly confronting catastrophic climate change.

Each of us comes to archaeology and its myriad methods and questions from a different background, and so each of us tells a different story of the past. Those stories do not negate each other but create a rich and complicated tapestry of knowledge, complete with hanging strings for the next generation to unravel or incorporate as they see fit. When we touch trowel to earth or open a box in a museum storeroom, we do so guided by our training but also by a motivation to better understand some corner of the human world, often one neglected by the wider public. Archaeology and its methods help us tell stories of the people and moments who are invisible to, forgotten by, or unimportant or shameful enough to be left out of written history. Even in our very networked, highly surveilled, and endlessly editorialised present, archaeological research into the detritus of everyday life allows us to surface and centre marginalised people and communities and push back against an inequitable status quo.

The archaeology I have been trained to do is worlds apart from that of Michener's mid-twentieth-century protagonist whose own approach would have been barely recognisable to the discipline's nineteenth-century practitioners. Today, archaeology is a team sport, requiring collaboration among a host of highly trained specialists and often motivated and shaped by close collaboration with local and descendant communities. The most exciting thing about a discipline that straddles so many fields, periods, communities, and

---

[223] Díaz-Andreu García (2007).

methods is that it can be directed at nearly any question to create new ways of understanding people, our societies, and the many ways we inhabit and experience the world. Like all the best stories, archaeological narratives do not just tell us how things once were but help us understand how they are now and might be in years to come. With an uncertain future before us, these sorts of stories are more important than ever.

References

Adkins, Lesley and Roy Adkins. 1989. *Archaeological Illustration*. Cambridge Manuals in Archaeology. Cambridge: Cambridge University Press.

Alpaslan-Roodenberg, Songül, David W. Anthony, Hiba Babiker et al. 2021. 'Ethics of DNA Research on Human Remains: Five Globally Applicable Guidelines'. *Nature* 599, no. 7883, 41–6. https://doi.org/10.1038/s41586-021-04008-x.

Arnold, Bettina. 1990. 'The Past As Propaganda: Totalitarian Archaeology in Nazi Germany'. *Antiquity* 64, no. 244, 464–78. https://doi.org/10.1017/S0003598X00078376.

Arnold, Bettina. 2006. '"Arierdämmerung": Race and Archaeology in Nazi Germany'. *World Archaeology* 38, no. 1, 8–31. www.jstor.org/stable/40023592.

Ash, Abigail, Michael Francken, Ildikó Pap et al. 2016. 'Regional Differences in Health, Diet and Weaning Patterns amongst the First Neolithic Farmers of Central Europe'. *Scientific Reports* 6, no. 1, 29458. https://doi.org/10.1038/srep29458.

Atalay, Sonya. 2012. *Community-Based Archaeology: Research With, By, and For Indigenous and Local Communities*. Berkeley: University of California Press.

Atalay, Sonya, Lee Rains Clauss, Randall H. McGuire, and John R. Welch. 2016. 'Transforming Archaeology'. In Sonya Atalay, Lee Rains Clauss, John R. Welch, and Randall H. McGuire (eds.), *Transforming Archaeology: Activist Practices and Prospects*. London: Routledge, pp. 7–28.

Atalay, Sonya, Lee Rains Clauss, John R. Welch, and Randall H. McGuire (eds.). 2016. *Transforming Archaeology: Activist Practices and Prospects*. London: Routledge.

Austen, Ian. 2021. 'How Thousands of Indigenous Children Vanished in Canada'. *New York Times* (7 June). www.nytimes.com/2021/06/07/world/canada/mass-graves-residential-schools.html.

Azkarate, Agustín. 2020. 'Archaeology of Architecture: Buildings Archaeology'. In Charles E. Orser, Andres Zarankin, Pedro P. A. Funari, Susan Lawrence, and James Symonds (eds.), *The Routledge Handbook of Global Historical Archaeology*. London: Routledge, pp. 517–35.

Ballard, Chris. 2016. 'The Legendary Roi Mata'. *Connexions* 4, 98–111.

Ballard, Chris. 2020. 'The Lizard in the Volcano: Narratives of the Kuwae Eruption'. *The Contemporary Pacific* 32, no. 1, 98–123.

Banning, E. B. 2002. *Archaeological Survey*. New York: Kluwer Academic/ Plenum Publishers.

Barwick, Linda. 2023. 'Songs and the Deep Present'. In Ann McGrath, Laura Rademaker, and Jakelin Troy (eds.), *Everywhen: Australia and the Language of Deep History*. Lincoln: University of Nebraska Press, pp. 93–122.

Bayliss, Alex. 2009. 'Rolling Out Revolution: Using Radiocarbon Dating in Archaeology'. *Radiocarbon* 51, no. 1, 123–47. https://doi.org/10.1017/S0033 822200033750.

Bayliss, Alex, Fachtna McAvoy, and Alasdair Whittle. 2007. 'The World Recreated: Redating Silbury Hill in Its Monumental Landscape'. *Antiquity* 81, no. 311, 26–53. https://doi.org/10.1017/S0003598X00094825.

Beck, Wendy and Margaret Somerville. 2005. 'Conversations between Disciplines: Historical Archaeology and Oral History at Yarrawarra'. *World Archaeology* 37, no. 3, 468–83. https://doi.org/10.1080/00438240500 204403.

Bennett, Jane. 2010. *Vibrant Matter: A Political Ecology of Things*. Durham, NC: Duke University Press.

Bergström, Anders, Chris Stringer, Mateja Hajdinjak, Eleanor M. L. Scerri, and Pontus Skoglund. 2021. 'Origins of Modern Human Ancestry'. *Nature* 590, no. 7845, 229–37. https://doi.org/10.1038/s41586-021-03244-5.

Bernbeck, Reinhard and Susan Pollock. 2007. '"Grabe, Wo Du Stehst!": An Archaeology of Perpetrators'. In Yannis Hamilakis and Philip Duke (eds.), *Archaeology and Capitalism: From Ethics to Politics*. London: Routledge, pp. 217–33.

Bibby, David I. 1993. 'Building Stratigraphic Sequences on Excavations: An Example from Konstanz, Germany. In Edward C. Harris, Marley R. Brown III, and Gregory J. Brown (eds.), *Practices of Archaeological Stratigraphy*. London: Academic Press, pp. 104–21.

Biers, Trish. 2019. 'Rethinking Purpose, Protocol, and Popularity in Displaying the Dead in Museums'. In Kirsty Squires, David Errickson, and Nicholas Márquez-Grant (eds.), *Ethical Approaches to Human Remains: A Global Challenge in Bioarchaeology and Forensic Anthropology*. Cham: Springer, pp. 239–63.

Bintliff, John L. 2000. 'The Concepts of "Site" and "Offsite" Archaeology in Surface Artefact Survey'. In Marinalle Pasquinucci and Frederic Trement (eds.), *Non-destructive Techniques Applied to Landscape Archaeology*. Oxford: Oxbow Books, pp. 200–15.

Black Trowel Collective. 2016. 'Foundations of an Anarchist Archaeology: A Community Manifesto'. *Savage Minds* (31 October). https://savageminds

.org/2016/10/31/foundations-of-an-anarchist-archaeology-a-community-manifesto/.

Black Trowel Collective. 2021. 'Archaeologists for Trans Liberation'. *anthro {dendum}* (6 August). https://anthrodendum.org/2021/08/06/archaeologists-for-trans-liberation/.

Booth, Thomas J. 2019. 'A Stranger in a Strange Land: A Perspective on Archaeological Responses to the Palaeogenetic Revolution from an Archaeologist Working amongst Palaeogeneticists'. *World Archaeology* 51, no. 4, 586–601. https://doi.org/10.1080/00438243.2019.1627240.

Booth, Thomas J., Joanna Brück, Selina Brace, and Ian Barnes. 2021. 'Tales from the Supplementary Information: Ancestry Change in Chalcolithic–Early Bronze Age Britain Was Gradual with Varied Kinship Organization'. *Cambridge Archaeological Journal* 31, no. 3, 379–400. https://doi.org/10.1017/S0959774321000019.

Borck, Lewis. 2019. 'Constructing the Future History: Prefiguration As Historical Epistemology and the Chronopolitics of Archaeology'. *Journal of Contemporary Archaeology* 5, no. 2, 229–38.

Borck, Lewis and Matthew C. Sanger. 2017. 'An Introduction to Anarchism and Archaeology'. *The SAA Archaeological Record* 17, no. 1, 9–16.

Boyd, Robert and Peter J. Richerson. 1985. *Culture and the Evolutionary Process*. Chicago, IL: University of Chicago Press.

Bracknell, Clint. 2023. 'Old Dogs and Ice Ages in Noongar Country'. In Ann McGrath, Laura Rademaker, and Jakelin Troy (eds.), *Everywhen: Australia and the Language of Deep History*. Lincoln, NE: University of Nebraska Press, pp. 75–92.

Bronk Ramsey, Christopher. 2009. 'Bayesian Analysis of Radiocarbon Dates'. *Radiocarbon* 51, no. 1, 337–60. https://doi.org/10.1017/S0033822200033865.

Bronk Ramsey, Christopher. 2017. 'Methods for Summarizing Radiocarbon Datasets'. *Radiocarbon* 59, no. 6, 1809–33. https://doi.org/10.1017/RDC.2017.108.

Brophy, Kenneth. 2018. 'The Brexit Hypothesis and Prehistory'. *Antiquity* 92, no. 366, 1650–8. https://doi.org/10.15184/aqy.2018.160.

Brophy, Kenneth. 2019. 'The Moggalithic Antiquarian: Party Political Broadcasts from Stone Circles'. *Almost Archaeology*. https://almostarchaeology.com/post/189644783963/moggalithic.

Bronk Ramsey, C. 2021. OxCal. v 4.4.4. https://c14.arch.ox.ac.uk/oxcal.html.

Brück, Joanna. 2021. 'Ancient DNA, Kinship and Relational Identities in Bronze Age Britain'. *Antiquity* 95, no. 379, 228–37. https://doi.org/10.15184/aqy.2020.216.

Bryden, Joan. 2021. 'Royal Assent Given to Bill Creating National Day for Truth and Reconciliation'. *CBC* (5 June). www.cbc.ca/news/canada/manitoba/national-day-truth-reconciliation-canada-passes-senate-1.6054847.

Cessford, Craig, Christiana L. Scheib, Meriam Guellil et al. 2021. 'Beyond Plague Pits: Using Genetics to Identify Responses to Plague in Medieval Cambridgeshire'. *European Journal of Archaeology* 24, no. 4, 496–518. https://doi.org/10.1017/eaa.2021.19.

Chapman, Robert. 2013. 'Death, Burial, and Social Representation'. In Sarah Tarlow and Liv Nilsson Stutz (eds.), *The Oxford Handbook of the Archaeology of Death and Burial*. Oxford: Oxford University Press, pp. 47–57.

Chapman, Robert and Alison Wylie. 2016. *Evidential Reasoning in Archaeology*. Debates in Archaeology. London: Bloomsbury Academic.

Childe, V. Gordon. 1925. *The Dawn of European Civilization*. London: A. A. Knopf.

Childe, V. Gordon. 1929. *The Danube in Prehistory*. Oxford: Clarendon Press.

Childe, V. Gordon. 1934. *New Light on the Most Ancient East: The Oriental Prelude to European Prehistory*. London: Kegan Paul, Trench, Trubner.

Chirikure, Shadreck. 2014. 'Land and Sea Links: 1500 Years of Connectivity between Southern Africa and the Indian Ocean Rim Regions, AD 700 to 1700'. *African Archaeological Review* 31, no. 4, 705–24. https://doi.org/10.1007/s10437-014-9171-6.

Choin, Jeremy, Javier Mendoza-Revilla, Lara R. Arauna et al. 2021. 'Genomic Insights into Population History and Biological Adaptation in Oceania'. *Nature* 592, no. 7855, 583–9. https://doi.org/10.1038/s41586-021-03236-5.

Clarke, D. L. 1970. *Beaker Pottery of Great Britain and Ireland*. Cambridge: Cambridge University Press.

Claw, Katrina G., Matthew Z. Anderson, Rene L. Begay et al. 2018. 'A Framework for Enhancing Ethical Genomic Research with Indigenous Communities'. *Nature Communications* 9, no. 1, 2957. https://doi.org/10.1038/s41467-018-05188-3.

Colwell-Chanthaphonh, Chip, T. J. Ferguson, Dorothy Lippert et al. 2010. 'The Premise and Promise of Indigenous Archaeology'. *American Antiquity* 75, no. 2, 228–38. www.jstor.org/stable/25766193.

Conkey, Margaret W. and Joan M. Gero. 1997. 'Programme to Practice: Gender and Feminism in Archaeology'. *Annual Review of Anthropology* 26, 411–37. www.jstor.org/stable/2952529.

Cooper, Anwen, Duncan Garrow, Catriona Gibson, Melanie Giles, and Neil Wilkin. 2022. *Grave Goods: Objects and Death in Later Prehistoric Britain*. Oxford: Oxbow Books.

Costello, Andrew. 2021. 'Beyond the Shovel and the Sieve: Achieving Better Outcomes for Aboriginal People in Commercial Archaeology'. *Australasian Journal of Environmental Management* 28, no. 1, 45–58. https://doi.org/10.1080/14486563.2021.1894251.

Crellin, Rachel J. and Oliver J. T. Harris. 2020. 'Beyond Binaries. Interrogating Ancient DNA'. *Archaeological Dialogues* 27, no. 1, 37–56. https://doi.org/10.1017/S1380203820000082.

Crump, Sarah E. 2021. 'Sedimentary Ancient DNA As a Tool in Paleoecology'. *Nature Reviews Earth and Environment* 2, no. 4, 229. https://doi.org/10.1038/s43017-021-00158-8.

Currie, Adrian. 2018. *Rock, Bone, and Ruin: An Optimist's Guide to the Historical Sciences.* Life and Mind: Philosophical Issues in Biology and Psychology. Cambridge, MA: MIT Press.

Currie, Adrian. 2021. 'Stepping Forwards by Looking Back: Underdetermination, Epistemic Scarcity and Legacy Data'. *Perspectives on Science* 29, no. 1, 104–32.

Dawkins, Richard. 1976. *The Selfish Gene.* Oxford: Oxford University Press.

Dee, Michael W., David Wengrow, Andrew J. Shortland et al. 2014. 'Radiocarbon Dating and the Naqada Relative Chronology'. *Journal of Archaeological Science* 46, 319–23. https://doi.org/10.1016/j.jas.2014.03.016.

Deloria, Vine. 1992. 'Indians, Archaeologists, and the Future'. *American Antiquity* 57, no. 4, 595–8. https://doi.org/10.2307/280822.

Dethlefsen, Edwin and James Deetz. 1966. 'Death's Heads, Cherubs, and Willow Trees: Experimental Archaeology in Colonial Cemeteries'. *American Antiquity* 31, no. 4, 502–10. https://doi.org/10.2307/2694382.

Díaz-Andreu García, Margarita. 2007. *A World History of Nineteenth-Century Archaeology: Nationalism, Colonialism, and the Past.* Oxford: Oxford University Press.

Dobres, Marcia-Anne. 2000. *Technology and Social Agency: Outlining a Practice Framework for Archaeology.* Social Archaeology. Oxford: Blackwell.

Donoghue, Helen D. 2019. 'Tuberculosis and Leprosy Associated with Historical Human Population Movements in Europe and Beyond: An Overview Based on Mycobacterial Ancient DNA'. *Annals of Human Biology* 46, no. 2, 120–8. https://doi.org/10.1080/03014460.2019.1624822.

Dorrell, Peter G. 1994. *Photography in Archaeology and Conservation.* 2nd ed. Cambridge: Cambridge University Press.

Dowson, Thomas A. 2000. 'Why Queer Archaeology? An Introduction'. *World Archaeology* 32, no. 2, 161–5. https://doi.org/10.1080/00438240050131144.

Duday, Henri, Anna Maria Cipriani, and John Pearce. 2009. *The Archaeology of the Dead: Lectures in Archaeothanatology*. Oxford: Oxbow Books.

Dunnell, Robert C. 1980. 'Evolutionary Theory and Archaeology'. *Advances in Archaeological Method and Theory* 3, 35–99.

Durvasula, Arun and Sriram Sankararaman. 2020. 'Recovering Signals of Ghost Archaic Introgression in African Populations'. *Science Advances* 6, no. 7, eaax5097. https://doi.org/10.1126/sciadv.aax5097.

Evans, Christopher. 2014. 'Soldiering Archaeology: Pitt Rivers and "Militarism"'. *Bulletin of the History of Archaeology* 24, no. 4, 1–20. https://doi.org/10.5334/bha.244.

Evans, Linda and Anna-Latifa Mourad. 2018. 'Dstretch® and Egyptian Tomb Paintings: A Case Study from Beni Hassan'. *Journal of Archaeological Science: Reports* 18, 78–84. https://doi.org/10.1016/j.jasrep.2018.01.011.

Fernández, Jesús, Gabriel Moshenska, and Eneko Iriarte. 2019. 'Archaeology and Climate Change: Evidence of a Flash-Flood during the LIA in Asturias (NW Spain) and Its Social Consequences'. *Environmental Archaeology* 24, no. 1, 38–48. https://doi.org/10.1080/14614103.2017.1407469.

Fforde, Cressida. 2004. *Collecting the Dead: Archaeology and the Reburial Issue*. London: Duckworth.

Fisher, Chelsea. 2020. 'Archaeology for Sustainable Agriculture'. *Journal of Archaeological Research* 28, no. 3, 393–441. https://doi.org/10.1007/s10814-019-09138-5.

Fisher, Lisa Jayne. 2009a. *Photography for Archaeologists Part I: Site Specific Record*. BAJR [British Archaeological Jobs Resource] Practical Guide Series, No. 25. www.bajr.org/BAJRGuides/25.%20Site%20Specific%20Photography/25PhotographyforArchaeologists.pdf.

Fisher, Lisa Jayne. 2009b. *Photography for Archaeologists Part II: Artefact Recording*. BAJR [British Archaeological Jobs Resource] Practical Guide Series, No. 26. www.bajr.org/BAJRGuides/26.%20Artefact%20Photography%20in%20Archaeology/26ArtefactPhotographyforArchaeologists.pdf.

Flexner, James L. 2014. 'The Historical Archaeology of States and Non-States: Anarchist Perspectives from Hawai'I and Vanuatu'. *Journal of Pacific Archaeology* 5, no. 2, 81–97.

Flexner, James L. 2020a. 'Anarchist Theory in the Pacific and "Pacific Anarchists" in Archaeological Thought'. In Tim Thomas (ed.), *Theory in the Pacific, the Pacific in Theory: Archaeological Perspectives*. London: Routledge, pp. 200–16.

Flexner, James L. 2020b. 'Degrowth and a Sustainable Future for Archaeology'. *Archaeological Dialogues* 27, no. 2, 159–71. https://doi.org/10.1017/S1380203820000203.

Fox, Keolu and John Hawkes. 2019. 'Use Ancient Remains More Wisely'. *Nature* 572, 581–3.https://doi.org/10.1038/d41586-019-02516-5.

Franklin, Maria. 1997. 'Why Are There So Few Black American Archaeologists?' *Antiquity* 71, no. 274, 799–801. https://doi.org/10.1017/S0003598X00085732.

Franklin, Maria, Justin P. Dunnavant, Ayana Omilade Flewellen et al. 2020. 'The Future Is Now: Archaeology and the Eradication of Anti-Blackness'. *International Journal of Historical Archaeology* 24, no. 4, 753–66. https://doi.org/10.1007/s10761-020-00577-1.

Frieman, Catherine J. 2021. *An Archaeology of Innovation: Approaching Social and Technological Change in Human Society.* Manchester: Manchester University Press.

Frieman, Catherine J. 2023. 'Innovation, Continuity and the Punctuated Temporality of Archaeological Narratives'. In Ann McGrath, Laura Rademaker, and Jakelin Troy (eds.), *Everywhen: Australia and the Language of Deep History.* Lincoln: University of Nebraska Press, pp. 195–220.

Frieman, Catherine J. and Daniela Hofman. 2019. 'Present Pasts in the Archaeology of Genetics, Identity, and Migration in Europe: A Critical Essay'. *World Archaeology* 51, no. 4, 528–45. https://doi.org/10.1080/00438243.2019.1627907.

Frieman, Catherine J. and James Lewis. 2022. 'Trickle Down Innovation? Creativity and Innovation at the Margins'. *World Archaeology* 53, no. 5, 723–40.

Frieman, Catherine J., Anne Teather, and Chelsea Morgan. 2019. 'Bodies in Motion: Narratives and Counter Narratives of Gendered Mobility in European Later Prehistory'. *Norwegian Archaeological Review* 52, no. 2, 148–69. https://doi.org/10.1080/00293652.2019.1697355.

Gannon, Megan I. 2020. 'Unearthing the True Toll of the Tulsa Race Massacre'. *Sapiens* (22 May). www.sapiens.org/news/tulsa-race-massacre/.

Gell, Alfred. 1992. *The Anthropology of Time: Cultural Constructions of Temporal Maps and Images.* Oxford: Berg.

Geller, Pamela L. 2020. 'Building Nation, Becoming Object: The Bio-Politics of the Samuel G. Morton Crania Collection'. *Historical Archaeology* 54, no. 1, 52–70. https://doi.org/10.1007/s41636-019-00218-3.

Gero, Joan M. 1985. 'Socio-Politics and the Woman-at-Home Ideology'. *American Antiquity* 50, no. 2, 342–50.

Gero, Joan M. 2007. 'Honoring Ambiguity/Problematizing Certitude'. *Journal of Archaeological Method and Theory* 14, no. 3, 311–27. https://doi.org/10.1007/s10816-007-9037-1.

Gillespie, Susan D. 2011. 'Archaeological Drawings As Re-presentations: The Maps of Complex A, La Venta, Mexico'. *Latin American Antiquity* 22, no. 1, 3–36. https://doi.org/10.7183/1045–6635.22.1.3.

Gillings, Mark, Piraye Hacigüzeller, and Gary R. Lock, (eds.). 2018. *Re-mapping Archaeology: Critical Perspectives, Alternative Mappings*. London: Routledge.

Gillings, Mark, Piraye Hacigüzeller, and Gary R. Lock, (eds.). 2020. *Archaeological Spatial Analysis: A Methodological Guide*. Abingdon: Routledge.

Gillings, Mark, Joshua Pollard, David Wheatley et al. 2008. *Landscape of the Megaliths: Excavation and Fieldwork on the Avebury Monuments, 1997–2003*. Oxford: Oxbow.

Goldhahn, Joakim, Linda Biyalwanga, Sally K. May et al. 2021. '"Our Dad's Painting Is Hiding, in Secret Place": Reverberations of a Rock Painting Episode in Kakadu National Park, Australia'. *Rock Art Research* 38, no. 1, 59–69. https://doi.org/10.3316/informit.039757093101317.

Goldhahn, Joakim, Sally K. May, Josie Gumbuwa Maralngurra et al. 2020. 'Children and Rock Art: A Case Study from Western Arnhem Land, Australia'. *Norwegian Archaeological Review* 53, no. 1, 59–82. https://doi.org/10.1080/00293652.2020.1779802.

Gonzalez, Sara L. and Briece Edwards. 2020. 'The Intersection of Indigenous Thought and Archaeological Practice: The Field Methods in Indigenous Archaeology Field School'. *Journal of Community Archaeology and Heritage* 7, no. 4, 239–54. https://doi.org/10.1080/20518196.2020.1724631.

González-Ruibal, Alfredo. 2008. 'Time to Destroy: An Archaeology of Supermodernity'. *Current Anthropology* 49, no. 2, 247–79. https://doi.org/10.1086/526099.

González-Ruibal, Alfredo. 2019. *An Archaeology of the Contemporary Era*. Abingdon: Routledge.

González-Tennant, Edward. 2018. *The Rosewood Massacre: An Archaeology and History of Intersectional Violence*. Cultural Heritage Studies. Gainesville: University Press of Florida.

Goodrum, Matthew R. 2009. 'The History of Human Origins Research and Its Place in the History of Science: Research Problems and Historiography'. *History of Science* 47, no. 3, 337–57. https://doi.org/10.1177/0073275309 04700305.

Goude, G., I. Dori, V. S. Sparacello et al. 2020. 'Multi-Proxy Stable Isotope Analyses of Dentine Microsections Reveal Diachronic Changes in Life History Adaptations, Mobility, and Tuberculosis-Induced Wasting in Prehistoric Liguria (Finale Ligure, Italy, Northwestern Mediterranean)'.

International Journey of Paleopathology 28, 99–111. https://doi.org/10 .1016/j.ijpp.2019.12.007.

Gräslund, Bo. 1987. *The Birth of Prehistoric Chronology: Dating Methods and Dating Systems in Nineteenth-Century Scandinavian Archaeology.* New Studies in Archaeology. Cambridge: Cambridge University Press.

Grauer, Anne L. 2018. 'A Century of Paleopathology'. *American Journal of Physical Anthropology* 165, no. 4, 904–14. https://doi.org/10.1002/ajpa.23366.

Graves-Brown, Paul, Clive Gamble, and Sian Jones (eds.). 1996. *Cultural Identity and Archaeology: The Construction of European Communities.* Theoretical Archaeology Group (Tag). London: Routledge.

Grono, Elle, David E. Friesem, Thi My Dzung Lam et al. 2022. 'Microstratigraphy Reveals Cycles of Occupation and Abandonment at the Mid Holocene Coastal Site of Thach Lac, Northern-Central Vietnam'. *Archaeological Research in Asia* 31, 100396. https://doi.org/10.1016/j.ara.2022.100396.

Grono, Elle, David E. Friesem, Rachel Wood et al. 2022. 'Site Formation Processes of Outdoor Spaces in Tropical Environments: A Micro-Geoarchaeological Case Study from Backyard Lo Gach, Southern Vietnam'. *Archaeological and Anthropological Sciences* 14, no. 11, 211. https://doi.org/10.1007/s12520-022-01666-4.

Grono, Elle, Philip J. Piper, Khanh Trung Kien Nguyen et al. 2022. 'The Identification of Dwellings and Site Formation Processes at Archaeological Settlements in the Tropics: A Micro-Geoarchaeological Case Study from Neolithic Loc Giang, Southern Vietnam'. *Quaternary Science Reviews* 291, 107654. https://doi.org/10.1016/j.quascirev.2022.107654.

Haglund, William D., Melissa Connor, and Douglas D. Scott. 2001. 'The Archaeology of Contemporary Mass Graves'. *Historical Archaeology* 35, no. 1, 57–69. https://doi.org/10.1007/BF03374527.

Hakenbeck, Susanne E. 2019. 'Genetics, Archaeology and the Far Right: An Unholy Trinity'. *World Archaeology* 51, no. 4, 517–27. https://doi.org/ 10.1080/00438243.2019.1617189.

Härke, Heinrich. 2014. 'Archaeology and Nazism: A Warning from Prehistory'. In Valentina Mordvintseva, Heinrich Härke, and Tetyana Shevchenko (eds.), *Archaeological and Linguistic Research: Materials of the Humboldt-Conference (Simferopol–Yalta, 20–23 September, 2012), Kiev.* Kiev: Stilos, pp. 32–43.

Harris, Edward C. 1979. *Principles of Archaeological Stratigraphy.* Studies in Archaeological Science. London: Academic Press.

Hawkes, Christopher. 1954. 'Archaeological Theory and Method: Some Suggestions from the Old World'. *American Anthropologist* 56, no. 2, 155–68.

Hicks, Dan. 2010. 'The Material-Cultural Turn: Event and Effect'. In Dan Hicks and Mary C. Beaudry (eds.), *The Oxford Handbook of Material Culture Studies*. Oxford: Oxford University Press, pp. 25–98.

Hodder, Ian. 1999. *The Archaeological Process: An Introduction*. Oxford: Blackwell.

Hodder, Ian. 2012. *Entangled: An Archaeology of the Relationships between Humans and Things*. Oxford: Wiley-Blackwell.

Hodgetts, Sharon and Jesse Hodgetts. 2020. 'Putting the Social Back into Archaeology'. *Australian Archaeology* 86, no. 3, 304–5. https://doi.org/10.1080/03122417.2020.1834186.

Hofmann, Daniela, Emily Hanscam, Martin Furholt et al. 2021. 'Forum: Populism, Identity Politics and the Archaeology of Europe'. *European Journal of Archaeology* 24, no. 4, 519–55. https://doi.org/10.1017/eaa.2021.29.

Hogg, Alan G., Timothy J. Heaton, Quan Hua et al. 2020. 'Shcal20 Southern Hemisphere Calibration, 0–55,000 Years Cal Bp'. *Radiocarbon* 62, no. 4, 759–78. https://doi.org/10.1017/RDC.2020.59.

Hornstrup, Karen Margrethe, Jesper Olsen, Jan Heinemeier et al. 2012. 'A New Absolute Danish Bronze Age Chronology As Based on Radiocarbon Dating of Cremated Bone Samples from Burials'. *Acta Archaeologica* 83, no. 1, 9–53. https://doi.org/10.1111/j.1600-0390.2012.00513.x.

Hudson, Mark J., Mami Aoyama, Kara C. Hoover et al. 2012. 'Prospects and Challenges for an Archaeology of Global Climate Change'. *WIREs Climate Change* 3, no. 4, 313–28. https://doi.org/10.1002/wcc.174.

Irving, Terry. 2020. *The Fatal Lure of Politics: The Life and Thought of Vere Gordon Childe*. Melbourne: Monash University Publishing.

Jackson, Rowan C., Andrew J. Dugmore, and Felix Riede. 2018. 'Rediscovering Lessons of Adaptation from the Past'. *Global Environmental Change* 52, 58–65. https://doi.org/10.1016/j.gloenvcha.2018.05.006.

Johnston, Dave. 2004. 'Australian Indigenous Archaeology: Where's Our Mob At?' *The Artefact: The Journal of the Archaeological and Anthropological Society of Victoria* 27, 8–10.

Jones, Andrew Meirion, Andrew Cochrane, Chris Carter et al. 2015. 'Digital Imaging and Prehistoric Imagery: A New Analysis of the Folkton Drums'. *Antiquity* 89, no. 347, 1083–95. https://doi.org/10.15184/aqy.2015.127.

Jones, Siân and Lynette Russell. 2012. 'Archaeology, Memory and Oral Tradition: An Introduction'. *International Journal of Historical Archaeology* 16, no. 2, 267–83. https://doi.org/10.1007/s10761-012-0177-y.

Joy, Jody. 2009. 'Reinvigorating Object Biography: Reproducing the Drama of Object Lives'. *World Archaeology* 41, no. 4, 540–56. https://doi.org/10.1080/00438240903345530.

Kiddey, Rachael. 2017. *Homeless Heritage: Collaborative Social Archaeology As Therapeutic Practice*. Oxford: Oxford University Press.

Kiddey, Rachael. 2020. 'I'll Tell You What I Want, What I Really, Really Want! Open Archaeology That Is Collaborative, Participatory, Public, and Feminist'. *Norwegian Archaeological Review* 53, no. 1, 23–40. https://doi.org/10.1080/00293652.2020.1749877.

Knüsel, Christopher and Eline M. Schotsmans (eds.). 2021. *The Routledge Handbook of Archaeothanatology*. London: Routledge.

Koolmatrie, Jacinta. 2020. 'Destruction of Juukan Gorge: We Need to Know the History of Artefacts, But It Is More Important to Keep Them in Place'. *The Conversation* (2 June). https://theconversation.com/destruction-of-juukan-gorge-we-need-to-know-the-history-of-artefacts-but-it-is-more-important-to-keep-them-in-place-139650.

Košir, Uroš. 2020. 'When Violins Fell Silent: Archaeological Traces of Mass Executions of Romani People in Slovenia'. *European Journal of Archaeology* 23, no. 2, 250–71. https://doi.org/10.1017/eaa.2019.58.

Kossinna, Gustaf. 1928. *Ursprung Und Verbreitung Der Germanen in Vor- Und Frühgeschichtlicher Zeit*. Mannus-Bibliothek. Leipzig: Verlag von Curt Kabitzsch.

Kuhn, Steven L. 2020. *The Evolution of Paleolithic Technologies*. London: Routledge.

Kuitems, Margot, Birgitta L. Wallace, Charles Lindsay et al. 2021. 'Evidence for European Presence in the Americas in AD 1021'. *Nature* 601, 388–91. https://doi.org/10.1038/s41586-021-03972-8.

Laluk, Nicholas C., Lindsay M. Montgomery, Rebecca Tsosie et al. 2022. 'Archaeology and Social Justice in Native America'. *American Antiquity* 87, no. 4, 659–82. https://doi.org/10.1017/aaq.2022.59.

Lane, Christine S., David J. Lowe, Simon P. E. Blockley, Takehiko Suzuki, and Victoria C. Smith. 2017. 'Advancing Tephrochronology As a Global Dating Tool: Applications in Volcanology, Archaeology, and Palaeoclimatic Research'. *Quaternary Geochronology* 40, 1–7. https://doi.org/10.1016/j.quageo.2017.04.003.

Langford, R. F. 1983. 'Our Heritage – Your Playground'. *Australian Archaeology* no. 16, 1–6. http://www.jstor.org/stable/40286421.

Larsen, Clark Spencer, Simon W. Hillson, Başak Boz et al. 2015. 'Bioarchaeology of Neolithic Çatalhöyük: Lives and Lifestyles of an Early

Farming Society in Transition'. *Journal of World Prehistory* 28, no. 1, 27–68. https://doi.org/10.1007/s10963-015-9084-6.

Larsen, Clark Spencer, Christopher J. Knüsel, Scott D. Haddow et al. 2019. 'Bioarchaeology of Neolithic Çatalhöyük Reveals Fundamental Transitions in Health, Mobility, and Lifestyle in Early Farmers'. *Proceedings of the National Academy of Sciences* 116, no. 26, 12615–23. https://doi.org/10.1073/pnas.1904345116.

Latour, Bruno and Steve Woolgar. 1979. *Laboratory Life: The Social Construction of Scientific Facts*. Sage Library of Social Research. Beverly Hills, CA: Sage Publications.

Leakey, Mary D. 1979. *Olduvai Gorge: My Search for Early Man*. London: Collins.

Leary, Jim, David Field, and Gill Campbell (eds.). 2013. *Silbury Hill: The Largest Prehistoric Mound in Europe*. Swindon: English Heritage.

Leighton, Mary. 2015. 'Excavation Methodologies and Labour As Epistemic Concerns in the Practice of Archaeology: Comparing Examples from British and Andean Archaeology'. *Archaeological Dialogues* 22, no. 1, 65–88. https://doi.org/10.1017/S1380203815000100.

Lemonnier, Pierre. 1992. *Elements for an Anthropology of Technology*. Ann Arbor: University of Michigan Museum of Anthropological Archaeology.

Leroi-Gourhan, A. 1964. *Le geste et la parole, Vol. 1: Technique et langage*. Paris: Albin Michel.

Lewis, Carenza, Heleen van Londen, Arkadiusz Marciniak et al. 2022. 'Exploring the Impact of Participative Place-Based Community Archaeology in Rural Europe: Community Archaeology in Rural Environments Meeting Societal Challenges'. *Journal of Community Archaeology and Heritage* 9, no. 4, 267–86. https://doi.org/10.1080/20518196.2021.2014697.

Lewis, James and Catherine J. Frieman. 2017. *A Geophysical Survey of Talland Barton Enclosures, Field System and Hendersick Barrow, Talland, Cornwall*. Southeast Kernow Archaeological Survey, Report No. 8.

Libby, Willard F. 1946. 'Atmospheric Helium Three and Radiocarbon from Cosmic Radiation'. *Physical Review* 69, no. 11–12, 671–2. https://doi.org/10.1103/PhysRev.69.671.2.

Librado, Pablo, Naveed Khan, Antoine Fages et al. 2021. 'The Origins and Spread of Domestic Horses from the Western Eurasian Steppes'. *Nature* 598, no. 7882, 634–40. https://doi.org/10.1038/s41586-021-04018-9.

Liebelt, Belinda G. 2019. 'Touching Grindstones in Archaeological and Cultural Heritage Practice: Materiality, Affect and Emotion in Settler-Colonial Australia'. *Australian Archaeology* 85, no. 3, 267–78. https://doi.org/10.1080/03122417.2019.1751982.

Lipson, Mark, Pontus Skoglund, Matthew Spriggs et al. 2018. 'Population Turnover in Remote Oceania Shortly after Initial Settlement'. *Current Biology* 28, no. 7, 1157–65.e7. https://doi.org/10.1016/j.cub.2018.02.051.

Liu, Yue-Chen, Rosalind Hunter-Anderson, Olivia Cheronet et al. 2022. 'Ancient DNA Reveals Five Streams of Migration into Micronesia and Matrilocality in Early Pacific Seafarers'. *Science* 377, no. 6601, 72–9. https://doi.org/10.1126/science.abm6536.

Livingstone, Josephine. 2017. 'Racism, Medievalism, and the White Supremacists of Charlottesville'. *The New Republic* (16 August).

Lowe, David J., Peter M. Abbott, Takehiko Suzuki, and Britta J. L. Jensen. 2022. 'Global Tephra Studies: Role and Importance of the International Tephra Research Group "Commission on Tephrochronology" in Its First 60 Years'. *History of Geo- and Space Sciences* 13, no. 2, 93–132. https://doi.org/10.5194/hgss-13-93-2022.

Lucquin, Alexandre, Kevin Gibbs, Junzo Uchiyama et al. 2016. 'Ancient Lipids Document Continuity in the Use of Early Hunter–Gatherer Pottery through 9,000 Years of Japanese Prehistory'. *Proceedings of the National Academy of Sciences* 113, no. 15, 3991–6. https://doi.org/10.1073/pnas.1522908113.

Lucquin, Alexandre, Harry K. Robson, Yvette Eley et al. 2018. 'The Impact of Environmental Change on the Use of Early Pottery by East Asian Hunter-Gatherers'. *Proceedings of the National Academy of Sciences* 115, no. 31, 7931–6. https://doi.org/10.1073/pnas.1803782115.

Lyman, R. Lee. 2010. 'What Taphonomy Is, What It Isn't, and Why Taphonomists Should Care About the Difference'. *Journal of Taphonomy* 8, no. 1, 1–16.

Madison, Paige. 2016. 'The Most Brutal of Human Skulls: Measuring and Knowing the First Neanderthal'. *The British Journal for the History of Science* 49, no. 3, 411–32. https://doi.org/10.1017/S0007087416000650.

Mate, Geraldine and Sean Ulm. 2021. 'Working in Archaeology in a Changing World: Australian Archaeology at the Beginning of the Covid-19 Pandemic'. *Australian Archaeology* 87, no. 3, 229–50. https://doi.org/10.1080/03122417.2021.1986651.

May, Sally K., Joakim Goldhahn, Laura Rademaker et al. 2021. 'Quilp's Horse: Rock Art and Artist Life-Biography in Western Arnhem Land, Australia'. *Rock Art Research* 32, no. 2, 211–21. https://doi.org/10.3316/informit.097332974289155.

May, Sally K., Josie Maralngurra, Iain Johnston et al. 2019. '"This Is My Father's Painting": A First-Hand Account of the Creation of the Most Iconic Rock Art in Kakadu National Park'. *Rock Art Research* 36, 199–213.

May, Sally K., Melissa Marshall, Inés Domingo Sanz et al. 2017. 'Reflections on the Pedagogy of Archaeological Field Schools within Indigenous Community Archaeology Programmes in Australia'. *Public Archaeology* 16, no. 3–4, 172–90. https://doi.org/10.1080/14655187.2018.1483123.

May, Sally K., Paul S. C. Taçon, Andrea Jalandoni et al. 2021. 'The Re-emergence of Nganaparru (Water Buffalo) into the Culture, Landscape and Rock Art of Western Arnhem Land'. *Antiquity* 95, no. 383, 1298–314. https://doi.org/10.15184/aqy.2021.107.

May, Sally K., Luke Taylor, Catherine J. Frieman et al. 2020. 'Survival, Social Cohesion and Rock Art: The Painted Hands of Western Arnhem Land, Australia'. *Cambridge Archaeological Journal* 30, no. 3, 491–510. https://doi.org/10.1017/S0959774320000104.

May, Sally K., Daryl Wesley, Joakim Goldhahn et al. 2017. 'Symbols of Power: The Firearm Paintings of Madjedbebe (Malakunanja Ii)'. *International Journal of Historical Archaeology* 21, no. 3, 690–707. https://doi.org/10.1007/s10761-017-0393-6.

McCullough, John M., Kathleen M. Heath, and Alexis M. Smith. 2015. 'Hemochromatosis: Niche Construction and the Genetic Domino Effect in the European Neolithic'. *Human Biology* 87, no. 1, 39–58. https://doi.org/10.13110/humanbiology.87.1.0039.

McGrath, Ann, Laura Rademaker, and Jakelin Troy, eds. 2023. *Everywhen: Australia and the Language of Deep History*. Lincoln: University of Nebraska Press.

McKechnie, Iain. 2015. 'Indigenous Oral History and Settlement Archaeology in Barkley Sound, Western Vancouver Island'. *BC Studies: The British Canadian Quarterly* 187, 193–228.

Menand, Louis. 2001. 'Morton, Agassiz, and the Origins of Scientific Racism in the United States'. *The Journal of Blacks in Higher Education*, no. 34, 110–13. https://doi.org/10.2307/3134139.

Michener, James A. 1965. *The Source: A Novel*. New York: Random House.

Miller, Daniel. 1985. *Artefacts As Categories: A Study of Ceramic Variability in Central India*. Cambridge: Cambridge University Press.

Miller, Daniel (ed.). 2005. *Materiality*. Durham, NC: Duke University Press.

Miller, Peter N. 2017. *History and Its Objects: Antiquarianism and Material Culture since 1500*. Ithaca, NY: Cornell University Press.

Mills, Barbara J. 2018. 'Intermarriage, Technological Diffusion, and Boundary Objects in the U.S. Southwest'. *Journal of Archaeological Method and Theory* 25, no. 4, 1051–86. https://doi.org/10.1007/s10816-018-9392-0.

Mills, Barbara J., Jeffery J. Clark, and Matthew A. Peeples. 2016. 'Migration, Skill, and the Transformation of Social Networks in the Pre-Hispanic Southwest'. *Economic Anthropology* 3, no. 2, 203–15. https://doi.org/10.1002/sea2.12060.

Mills, Barbara J., Jeffery J. Clark, Matthew A. Peeples et al. 2013. 'Transformation of Social Networks in the Late Pre-Hispanic US Southwest" *Proceedings of the National Academy of Sciences* 110, no. 15, 5785–90.

Montelius, Oscar. 1986. *Dating in the Bronze Age, with Special Reference to Scandinavia*. Translated by Helen Clarke. Stockholm: Kungl. Vitterhets historie och antikvitets akademien.

Montelius, Oscar. 1903. *Die Typologische Methode*. Stockholm: Im Selbstverlag des Verfassers.

Morgan, Colleen and Holly Wright. 2018. 'Pencils and Pixels: Drawing and Digital Media in Archaeological Field Recording'. *Journal of Field Archaeology* 43, no. 2, 136–51. https://doi.org/10.1080/00934690.2018.1428488.

Morgan, Lewis H. 1985 [1877]. *Ancient Society*. Tucson: University of Arizona Press.

Moser, Stephanie. 2012. 'Archaeological Visualization: Early Artifact Illustration and the Birth of the Archaeological Image'. In Ian Hodder (ed.), *Archaeological Theory Today*. Cambridge: Polity, pp. 292–322.

Moshenska, Gabriel and Shaun Shelly. 2020. 'Notes for an Archaeology of Discarded Drug Paraphernalia'. *Archaeology International* 23, no. 1, 104–21.

Munn, Nancy D. 1992. 'The Cultural Anthropology of Time: A Critical Essay'. *Annual Review of Anthropology* 21, no. 1, 93–123. https://doi.org/10.1146/annurev.an.21.100192.000521.

Nabokov, Peter. 2002. *A Forest of Time: American Indian Ways of History*. Cambridge: Cambridge University Press.

Naugler, Christopher. 2008. 'Hemochromatosis: A Neolithic Adaptation to Cereal Grain Diets'. *Medical Hypotheses* 70, no. 3, 691–2. https://doi.org/10.1016/j.mehy.2007.06.020.

Neale, Margo and Lynne Kelly. 2020. *Songlines: The Power and Promise*. Melbourne: Thames & Hudson and The National Museum of Australia.

Niklasson, Elisabeth and Herdis Hølleland. 2018. 'The Scandinavian Far-Right and the New Politicisation of Heritage'. *Journal of Social Archaeology* 18, no. 2, 121–48. https://doi.org/10.1177/1469605318757340.

Novembre, John, Toby Johnson, Katarzyna Bryc et al. 2008. 'Genes Mirror Geography within Europe'. *Nature* 456, no. 7218, 98–101. https://doi.org/10.1038/nature07331.

O'Brien, Michael J. and Stephen J. Shennan (eds.). 2010. *Innovation in Cultural Systems: Contributions from Evolutionary Anthropology.* Cambridge, MA: MIT Press.

O'Connor, Sue, Jane Balme, Ursula Frederick et al. 2022. 'Art in the Bark: Indigenous Carved Boab Trees (Adansonia Gregorii) in North-West Australia'. *Antiquity* 96, no. 390, 1574–91. https://doi.org/10.15184/aqy.2022.129.

O'Connor, Sue, Jane Balme, Mona Oscar et al. 2022. 'Memory and Performance: The Role of Rock Art in the Kimberley, Western Australia'. In Leslie F. Zubieta (ed.), *Rock Art and Memory in the Transmission of Cultural Knowledge.* Cham: Springer, pp. 147–70.

Okumura, Mercedes and Astolfo G. M. Araujo. 2014. 'Long-Term Cultural Stability in Hunter–Gatherers: A Case Study Using Traditional and Geometric Morphometric Analysis of Lithic Stemmed Bifacial Points from Southern Brazil'. *Journal of Archaeological Science* 45, 59–71. https://doi.org/10.1016/j.jas.2014.02.009.

Olivier, Laurent. 2011. *The Dark Abyss of Time: Archaeology and Memory.* Archaeology in Society Series. Lanham, MD: AltaMira Press.

Orser, Charles E. and Pedro P. A. Funari. 2001. 'Archaeology and Slave Resistance and Rebellion'. *World Archaeology* 33, no. 1, 61–72. https://doi.org/10.1080/00438240126646.

Orton, Clive and Mike Hughes. 2013. *Pottery in Archaeology.* 2nd ed. Cambridge Manuals in Archaeology. Cambridge: Cambridge University Press.

Papathanasiou, Anastasia. 2011. 'Health, Diet and Social Implications in Neolithic Greece from the Study of Human Osteological Material'. In Ron Pinhasi and Jay T. Stock (eds.), *Human Bioarchaeology of the Transition to Agriculture.* London: John Wiley and Sons, pp. 85–105.

Parcak, Sarah H. 2014. 'GIS, Remote Sensing, and Landscape Archaeology'. In *The Oxford Handbook of Topics in Archaeology.* Oxford: Oxford University Press. https://doi.org/10.1093/oxfordhb/9780199935413.013.11.

Parker Pearson, Michael. 1999. *The Archaeology of Death and Burial.* Stroud: Sutton.

Pelegrin, Jacques. 1990. 'Prehistoric Lithic Technology: Some Aspects of Research'. *Archaeological Review from Cambridge* 9, no. 1, 116–25.

Pétrequin, Pierre, Serge Cassen, Michel Errera et al. (eds.). 2012. *Jade: Grandes haches alpines du Néolithique européen, Ve au IVe millénaires av. J.-C.* Besançon: Presses Universitaires de Franche-Comté.

Pétrequin, Pierre, Serge Cassen, Estelle Gauthier et al. 2012. 'Typologie, chronologie et répartition des grandes haches alpines en Europe occidentale'.

In Pierre Pétrequin, Serge Cassen, Michel Errera et al. (eds.), *Jade: Grandes haches alpines du Néolithique européen, Ve au IVᵉ millénaires av. J.-C.* Besançon: Presses Universitaires de Franche-Comté, pp. 574–727.

Petrie, W. M. Flinders. 1899. 'Sequences in Prehistoric Remains'. *The Journal of the Anthropological Institute of Great Britain and Ireland* 29, no. 3/4, 295–301. https://doi.org/10.2307/2843012.

Pétursdóttir, Þóra. 2017. 'Climate Change? Archaeology and Anthropocene'. *Archaeological Dialogues* 24, no. 2, 175–205. https://doi.org/10.1017/S1380203817000216.

Piggott, Stuart. 1989. *Ancient Britons and the Antiquarian Imagination: Ideas from the Renaissance to the Regency.* London: Thames & Hudson.

Pluciennik, Mark. 1999. 'Archaeological Narratives and Other Ways of Telling'. *Current Anthropology* 40, no. 5, 653–78. https://doi.org/10.1086/300085.

Posth, Cosimo, Kathrin Nägele, Heidi Colleran et al. 2018. 'Language Continuity Despite Population Replacement in Remote Oceania'. *Nature Ecology and Evolution* 2, no. 4, 731–40. https://doi.org/10.1038/s41559-018-0498-2.

Prentiss, Anna Marie (ed.). 2019. *Handbook of Evolutionary Research in Archaeology.* Cham: Springer.

Rademaker, Laura. 2023. 'Time and Eternity: Aboriginal and Missionary Conversations about Temporality'. In Ann McGrath, Laura Rademaker, and Jakelin Troy (eds.), *Everywhen: Australia and the Language of Deep History.* Lincoln: University of Nebraska Press, pp. 253–72.

Reich, David. 2019. *Who We Are and How We Got Here: Ancient DNA and the New Science of the Human Past.* Oxford: Oxford University Press.

Reimer, Paula J., William E. N. Austin, Edouard Bard et al. 2020. 'The IntCal20 Northern Hemisphere Radiocarbon Age Calibration Curve (0–55 Cal kBP)'. *Radiocarbon* 62, no. 4, 725–57. https://doi.org/10.1017/RDC.2020.41.

Rice, Prudence M. 2015. *Pottery Analysis: A Sourcebook.* 2nd ed. Chicago, IL: University of Chicago Press.

Richardson, Lorna-Jane and Jaime Almansa-Sánchez. 2015. 'Do You Even Know What Public Archaeology Is? Trends, Theory, Practice, Ethics'. *World Archaeology* 47, no. 2, 194–211. https://doi.org/10.1080/00438243.2015.1017599.

Rick, Torben C. and Daniel H. Sandweiss. 2020. 'Archaeology, Climate, and Global Change in the Age of Humans'. *Proceedings of the National Academy of Sciences* 117, no. 15, 8250–3. https://doi.org/10.1073/pnas.2003612117.

Riede, Felix. 2014. 'Climate Models: Use Archaeology Record'. *Nature* 513, no. 7518, 315. https://doi.org/10.1038/513315c.

Rink, W. Jack, Jeroen W. Thompson, Larry M. Heaman et al. (eds.). 2015. *Encyclopedia of Scientific Dating Methods*. Encyclopedia of Earth Sciences Series. Dordrecht: Springer Reference.

Rizvi, Uzma Z. 2013. 'Creating Prehistory and Protohistory: Constructing Otherness and Politics of Contemporary Indigenous Populations in India'. In Peter R. Schmidt and Stephen A. Mrozowski (eds.), *The Death of Prehistory*. Oxford: Oxford University Press, pp. 141–58.

Rowley-Conwy, P. 2007. *From Genesis to Prehistory: The Archaeological Three Age System and Its Contested Reception in Denmark, Britain, and Ireland*. Oxford Studies in the History of Archaeology. Oxford: Oxford University Press.

Rutherford, Adam. 2022. *Control: The Dark History and Troubling Present of Eugenics*. London: Weidenfeld & Nicolson.

Sabloff, Jeremy A. 2008. *Archaeology Matters: Action Archaeology in the Modern World*. Walnut Creek, CA: Left Coast Press.

Saini, Angela. 2019. *Superior: The Return of Race Science*. London: 4th Estate.

Sánchez-Pardo, José C., Rebeca Blanco-Rotea, and Jorge Sanjurjo-Sánchez. 2017. 'The Church of Santa Comba De Bande and Early Medieval Iberian Architecture: New Chronological Results'. *Antiquity* 91, no. 358, 1011–26. https://doi.org/10.15184/aqy.2017.83.

Sarris, Apostolos, Tuna Kalayci, Ian Moffat et al. 2018. 'An Introduction to Geophysical and Geochemical Methods in Digital Geoarchaeology'. In Christoph Siart, Markus Forbriger, and Olaf Bubenzer (eds.), *Digital Geoarchaeology: New Techniques for Interdisciplinary Human-Environmental Research*. Cham: Springer, pp. 215–36.

Sayer, Duncan. 2020. *Early Anglo-Saxon Cemeteries: Kinship, Community and Identity*. Social Archaeology and Material Worlds. Manchester: Manchester University Press.

Scarre, Geoffrey. 2003. 'Archaeology and Respect for the Dead'. *Journal of Applied Philosophy* 20, no. 3, 237–49. www.jstor.org/stable/24355053.

Schauer, Peter, Stephen Shennan, Andrew Bevan et al. 2021. 'Cycles in Stone Mining and Copper Circulation in Europe 5500–2000 BC: A View from Space'. *European Journal of Archaeology* 24, no. 2, 204–25. https://doi .org/10.1017/eaa.2020.56.

Schiffer, Michael B. 1987. *Formation Processes of the Archaeological Record*. 1st ed. Albuquerque: University of New Mexico Press.

Schlanger, Nathan. 1994. 'Mindful Technology: Unleashing the *châine opératoire* for an Archaeology of the Mind'. In Colin Renfrew and Ezra Zubrow (eds.), *The Ancient Mind: Elements of Cognitive Archaeology*. Cambridge: Cambridge University Press, pp. 143–51.

Schnapp, Alain. 1996. *The Discovery of the Past: The Origins of Archaeology.* London: British Museum Press.

Semple, Sarah and Stuart Brookes. 2020. 'Necrogeography and Necroscapes: Living with the Dead'. *World Archaeology* 52, no. 1, 1–15. https://doi.org/ 10.1080/00438243.2020.1779434.

Shanks, Michael and Christopher Y. Tilley. 1987. *Re-constructing Archaeology: Theory and Practice.* New Studies in Archaeology. Cambridge: Cambridge University Press.

Shoda, Shinya. 2021. 'Seeking Prehistoric Fermented Food in Japan and Korea'. *Current Anthropology* 62, no. S24, S242–S55. https://doi.org/ 10.1086/715808.

Shoda, Shinya, Alexandre Lucquin, Jae-ho Ahn et al. 2017. 'Pottery Use by Early Holocene Hunter-Gatherers of the Korean Peninsula Closely Linked with the Exploitation of Marine Resources'. *Quaternary Science Reviews* 170, 164–73. https://doi.org/10.1016/j.quascirev.2017.06.032.

Shoda, Shinya, Alexandre Lucquin, Oksana Yanshina et al. 2020. 'Late Glacial Hunter-Gatherer Pottery in the Russian Far East: Indications of Diversity in Origins and Use'. *Quaternary Science Reviews* 229, 106124. https://doi.org/ 10.1016/j.quascirev.2019.106124.

Sidoroff, Maria-Louise. 2015. 'An Ethnoarchaeological Study of the Zizia Pottery Factory in Jizza, Jordan'. *Ethnoarchaeology* 7, no. 2, 86–113. https://doi.org/10.1179/1944289015Z.00000000029.

Skinner, Mark. 1987. 'Planning the Archaeological Recovery of Evidence from Recent Mass Graves'. *Forensic Science International* 34, no. 4, 267–87. https://doi.org/10.1016/0379-0738(87)90040-5.

Small, Thomas. 2013. *Archaeological Illustration: Small Finds.* BAJR [British Archaeological Jobs Resource] Practical Guide Series, No. 32. www.bajr .org/BAJRGuides/32.%20Archaeological%20Illustration%20-%20Small %20Finds/Guide32.pdf.

Smith, Claire, Heather Burke, Jordan Ralph et al. 2019. 'Pursuing Social Justice through Collaborative Archaeologies in Aboriginal Australia'. *Archaeologies* 15, no. 3, 536–69. https://doi.org/10.1007/s11759-019-09382-7.

Sofaer, Joanna R. 2006. *The Body As Material Culture: A Theoretical Osteoarchaeology.* Cambridge: Cambridge University Press.

Solari, Ana, Sergio F. S. M. da Silva, Anne Marie Pessis et al. 2022. 'Older Burial Disturbance: Postfunerary Manipulation of Graves and Corpses in Precontact Northeastern Brazil'. *Latin American Antiquity* 33, no. 4, 824–37. https://doi.org/10.1017/laq.2022.10.

Spriggs, Matthew and David Reich. 2019. 'An Ancient DNA Pacific Journey: A Case Study of Collaboration between Archaeologists and Geneticists'.

World Archaeology 51, no. 4, 620–39. https://doi.org/10.1080/00438243 .2019.1733069.

Squires, Kirsty, David Errickson, and Nicholas Márquez-Grant (eds.). 2019. *Ethical Approaches to Human Remains: A Global Challenge in Bioarchaeology and Forensic Anthropology*. Cham: Springer.

Stahl, Ann Brower. 2022. *Archaeology: Why It Matters*. Cambridge: Polity Press.

Steele, Caroline. 2008. 'Archaeology and the Forensic Investigation of Recent Mass Graves: Ethical Issues for a New Practice of Archaeology'. *Archaeologies* 4, no. 3, 414–28. https://doi.org/10.1007/s11759-008-9080-x.

Steeves, Paulette F. C. 2021. *The Indigenous Paleolithic of the Western Hemisphere*. Lincoln: University of Nebraska Press.

Steiner, Mélanie and Lindsay Allason-Jones. 2005. *Approaches to Archaeological Illustration: A Handbook*. York: Council for British Archaeology.

Steward, Julian H. 1955. *Theory of Culture Change: The Methodology of Multilinear Evolution*. Urbana: University of Illinois Press.

Stock, Jay T., Emma Pomeroy, Christopher B. Ruff et al. 2023. 'Long-Term Trends in Human Body Size Track Regional Variation in Subsistence Transitions and Growth Acceleration Linked to Dairying'. *Proceedings of the National Academy of Sciences of the United States of America* 120, no. 4, e2209482119. https://doi.org/10.1073/pnas.2209482119.

Stottman, M. Jay (ed.). 2010a. *Archaeologists As Activists: Can Archaeologists Change the World?* Tuscaloosa: University of Alabama Press.

Stottman, M. Jay. 2010b. ' Introduction: Archaeologists As Activists'. In M. Jay Stottman (ed.), *Archaeologists As Activists: Can Archaeologists Change the World?* Tuscaloosa: University of Alabama Press, pp. 1–16.

Stout, Adam. 2013. 'Cultural History, Race, and Peoples'. In Sarah Tarlow and Liv Nilsson Stutz (eds.), *The Oxford Handbook of the Archaeology of Death and Burial*. Oxford: Oxford University Press, pp. 17–26.

Stuiver, Minze and Hans E. Suess. 1966. 'On the Relationship between Radiocarbon Dates and True Sample Ages'. *Radiocarbon* 8, 534–40. https://doi.org/10.1017/S0033822200000345.

Supernant, Kisha. 2020a. 'From Haunted to Haunting: Métis Ghosts in the Past and Present'. In Sarah Surface-Evans, A. E. Garrison, and Kisha Supernant (eds.), *Blurring Timescapes, Subverting Erasure*. New York: Berghahn Books, pp. 85–104.

Supernant, Kisha. 2020b. 'Grand Challenge No. 1: Truth and Reconciliation. Archaeological Pedagogy, Indigenous Histories, and Reconciliation in Canada'. *Journal of Archaeology and Education* 4, no. 3. https://digitalcom mons.library.umaine.edu/jae/vol4/iss3/2/.

TallBear, Kimberly. 2018. 'Making Love and Relations Beyond Settler Sex and Family.'' In Adele E. Clarke and Donna Jeanne Haraway (eds.), *Making Kin Not Population*. Chicago, IL: Prickly Paradigm Press, pp. 145–64.

Tarlow, Sarah. 2006. 'Archaeological Ethics and the People of the Past'. In Chris Scarre and Geoffrey Scarre (eds.), *The Ethics of Archaeology: Philosophical Perspectives on Archaeological Practice*. Cambridge: Cambridge University Press, pp. 199–216.

Taylor, R. Ervin. 1985. 'The Beginnings of Radiocarbon Dating in American Antiquity: A Historical Perspective'. *American Antiquity* 50, no. 2, 309–25. https://doi.org/10.2307/280489.

Teixeira, João C., Guy S. Jacobs, Chris Stringer et al. 2021. 'Widespread Denisovan Ancestry in Island Southeast Asia but No Evidence of Substantial Super-Archaic Hominin Admixture'. *Nature Ecology and Evolution* 5, no. 5, 616–24. https://doi.org/10.1038/s41559-021-01408-0.

Trigger, Bruce G. 1984. 'Alternative Archaeologies: Nationalist, Colonialist, Imperialist'. *Man* 19, no. 3, 355–70. https://doi.org/10.2307/2802176.

Trigger, Bruce G. 2006. *A History of Archaeological Thought*. 2nd ed. Cambridge: Cambridge University Press.

Tsosie, Krystal S., Rene L. Begay, Keolu Fox et al. 2020. 'Generations of Genomes: Advances in Paleogenomics Technology and Engagement for Indigenous People of the Americas'. *Current Opinion in Genetics and Development* 62, 91–6. https://doi.org/10.1016/j.gde.2020.06.010.

Turner, Derek D. 2005. 'Local Underdetermination in Historical Science'. *Philosophy of Science* 72, no. 1, 209–30. https://doi.org/10.1086/426851.

Turner, Derek D. 2007. *Making Prehistory: Historical Science and the Scientific Realism Debate*. Cambridge: Cambridge University Press.

Tylor, Edward B. 1865. *Researches into the Early History of Mankind and the Development of Civilization*. London: John Murray.

US Department of the Interior. 2021. 'Secretary Haaland Announces Federal Indian Boarding School Initiative'. Press Release (22 June).

Van de Noort, Robert. 2011. 'Conceptualising Climate Change Archaeology'. *Antiquity* 85, no. 329, 1039–48. https://doi.org/10.1017/S0003598X000 68472.

Vandkilde, Helle, Uffe Rahbek, and Kaare Lund Rasmussen. 1996. 'Radiocarbon Dating and the Chronology of Bronze Age Southern Scandinavia'. *Acta Archaeologica* 67, 183–98.

Veit, Richard. 1997. 'A Case of Archaeological Amnesia: A Contextual Biography of Montroville Wilson Dickeson (1810–1882), Early American Archaeologist'. *Archaeology of Eastern North America* 25, 97–123. www.jstor.org/stable/40914419.

Voss, Barbara L. 2000. 'Feminisms, Queer Theories, and the Archaeological Study of Past Sexualities'. *World Archaeology* 32, no. 2, 180–92. https://doi .org/10.1002/9780470775981.ch3.

Voss, Barbara L. 2008. 'Sexuality Studies in Archaeology'. *Annual Review of Anthropology* 37, no. 1, 317–36. https://doi.org/10.1146/annurev.anthro .37.081407.085238.

Voss, Barbara L. and Eleanor Conlin Casella (eds.). 2012. *The Archaeology of Colonialism: Intimate Encounters and Sexual Effects*. Cambridge: Cambridge University Press.

Wade, Lizzie. 2019. 'Caribbean Excavation Offers Intimate Look at the Lives of Enslaved Africans'. *Science* (7 November). www.sciencemag.org/news/2019/ 11/caribbean-excavation-offers-intimate-look-lives-enslaved-africans.

Walker, Phillip L., Rhonda R. Bathurst, Rebecca Richman et al. 2009. 'The Causes of Porotic Hyperostosis and Cribra Orbitalia: A Reappraisal of the Iron-Deficiency-Anemia Hypothesis'. *American Journal of Physical Anthropology* 139, no. 2, 109–25. https://doi.org/10.1002/ajpa.21031.

Walsh, Matthew J., Samantha Reiter, Catherine J. Frieman et al. 2022. 'In the Company of Men: Alternative Masculine Gender Identities in the Nordic Bronze Age. Re-interpreting a Same-Sex Double-Grave from Karlstrup, Denmark'. In Anna Tornberg, Andreas Svensson, and Jan Apel (eds.), *Life and Afterlife in the Nordic Bronze Age: Proceedings of the 15th Nordic Bronze Age Symposium Held in Lund, Sweden, June 11–15, 2019*. Lund: Lund University Press, pp. 159–82.

Watson, Richard A. 1990. 'Ozymandias, King of Kings: Postprocessual Radical Archaeology As Critique'. *American Antiquity* 55, no. 4, 673–89. https://doi .org/10.2307/281245.

Weismantel, Mary. 2013. 'Towards a Transgender Archaeology: A Queer Rampage through Prehistory'. In Susan Stryker and Aren Z. Aizura (eds.), *The Transgender Studies Reader 2*. London: Routledge, pp. 319–34.

Whelan, Aubrey and Zoe Greenberg. 2022. 'Penn Museum Seeks to Rebury Stolen Skulls of Black Philadelphians and Ignites Pushback'. *Philadelphia Inquirer* (6 August). https://web.archive.org/web/20220806000943/https:// www.inquirer.com/news/penn-museum-morton-skull-collection-burial- 20220805.html.

White, Leslie A. 1959. *The Evolution of Culture: The Development of Civilization to the Fall of Rome*. New York: McGraw-Hill.

White, William and Catherine Draycott. 2020. 'Why the Whiteness of Archaeology Is a Problem'. *Sapiens* (7 July). www.sapiens.org/archae ology/archaeology-diversity/.

Wilson, Edward O. 1975. *Sociobiology: The New Synthesis*. Cambridge, MA: Belknap Press of Harvard University Press.

Wiseman, James and Farouk El-Baz. 2007. *Remote Sensing in Archaeology*. New York: Springer.

Wittwer-Backofen, Ursula and Nicolas Tomo. 2008. 'From Health to Civilization Stress? In Search for Traces of a Health Transition during the Early Neolithic in Europe'. In Jean-Pierre Bocquet-Appel and Ofer Bar-Yosef (eds.), *The Neolithic Demographic Transition and Its Consequences*. Dordrecht: Springer, pp. 501–38.

Wood, James W., George R. Milner, Henry C. Harpending et al. 1992. 'The Osteological Paradox: Problems of Inferring Prehistoric Health from Skeletal Samples [and Comments and Reply]'. *Current Anthropology* 33, no. 4, 343–70. www.jstor.org/stable/2743861.

Wood, Rachel E., Alvaro Arrizabalaga, Marta Camps et al. 2014. 'The Chronology of the Earliest Upper Palaeolithic in Northern Iberia: New Insights from L'arbreda, Labeko Koba and La Viña'. *Journal of Human Evolution* 69, 91–109. https://doi.org/10.1016/j.jhevol.2013.12.017.

Wood, Rachel, Zenobia Jacobs, Dorcas Vannieuwenhuyse et al. 2016. 'Towards an Accurate and Precise Chronology for the Colonization of Australia: The Example of Riwi, Kimberley, Western Australia'. *PLOS ONE* 11, no. 9, e0160123. https://doi.org/10.1371/journal.pone.0160123.

Woolf, Daniel R. 1997. 'A Feminine Past? Gender, Genre, and Historical Knowledge in England, 1500–1800'. *The American Historical Review* 102, no. 3, 645–79. https://doi.org/10.1086/ahr/102.3.645.

Woolf, Daniel R. 2003. *The Social Circulation of the Past: English Historical Culture, 1500–1730*. Oxford: Oxford University Press.

Worsaae, Jens Jurgen A. 1849. *The Primeval Antiquities of Denmark*. Translated by William J. Thoms. London: John Henry Parker.

Zorzin, Nicolas. 2021. 'Is Archaeology Conceivable within the Degrowth Movement?' *Archaeological Dialogues* 28, no. 1, 1–16. https://doi.org/10.1017/S1380203821000015.

Cambridge Elements ⬄

Historical Theory and Practice

Daniel Woolf
Queen's University, Ontario

Daniel Woolf is Professor of History at Queen's University, where he served for ten years as Principal and Vice-Chancellor, and has held academic appointments at a number of Canadian universities. He is the author or editor of several books and articles on the history of historical thought and writing, and on early modern British intellectual history, including most recently *A Concise History of History* (CUP 2019). He is a Fellow of the Royal Historical Society, the Royal Society of Canada, and the Society of Antiquaries of London. He is married with 3 adult children.

About the Series
Cambridge Elements in Historical Theory and Practice is a series intended for a wide range of students, scholars, and others whose interests involve engagement with the past. Topics include the theoretical, ethical, and philosophical issues involved in doing history, the interconnections between history and other disciplines and questions of method, and the application of historical knowledge to contemporary global and social issues such as climate change, reconciliation and justice, heritage, and identity politics.

Cambridge Elements ≡

Historical Theory and Practice

Printed in the United States
by Baker & Taylor Publisher Services